FROM
SARAJEVO
TO
POTSDAM

18s.

IN U.K. ONLY

FROM SARAJEVO TO POTSDAM

A. J. P. TAYLOR

THAMES AND HUDSON · LONDON

© THAMES AND HUDSON 1966

PRINTED IN GREAT BRITAIN BY JARROLD AND SONS LTD NORWICH

CONTENTS

DEFINITIONS   7

I WAR   9

II POST-WAR   59

III PRE-WAR   119

IV WAR   159

BIBLIOGRAPHICAL NOTES   200

LIST OF ILLUSTRATIONS   203

INDEX   209

MAPS
    Europe before and after the First World War   10–11
    Europe before and after World War II   199

'European civilization' is not an easy assignment. Conventionally, Europe extends from the seas and oceans to the Urals, a geographic line of little significance. Bismarck asked, 'What is Europe?' and received the answer: 'Many great nations.' Some nations are more consciously European, some less. When an Englishman, for instance, says that he is going to 'Europe' for a holiday, he does not mean Stratford-on-Avon or even Edinburgh. Russians talk about 'the west' in the same way. However much we insist that Englishmen and Russians are Europeans, we tend to assume that 'the Continent' also exists in a narrower sense. Again, many of our generalizations apply only to western Europe, and more specifically to its wealthier classes. I have been disturbed by the question: 'Does this apply to a poor man in Warsaw as well as to a rich one in London or Paris?' I can only reply: 'No, but it soon will.' Culturally, the only precise and accurate definition of Europe is 'the area which uses the major and minor diatonic scale'. This is not much use in practice.

'Civilization' is more troublesome still. We usually mean by it moral, peaceful behaviour, or the fancier bits of life – art, literature, and central heating. The *Shorter Oxford Dictionary* gives '1. The assimilation of the Common Law to the Civil Law. 2. The action or process of civilizing or being civilized. 3. (More usually) civilized condition or state.' This is not helpful. The *Concise Oxford Dictionary* is a little better: 'Stage, esp. advanced stage, in social development.' I interpret civilization to mean the prevailing patterns of communal life, what men do in public. Probably I have not got the proportions right. John Nash, the architect, often neglected to put a scale on his drawings. The builder of Gloucester Terrace made the cornice twice the size which Nash had in mind. Nash only commented: 'It has come out rather big.' In the same way, this book has come out rather political. I can only plead that politics, in the widest sense, had

7

1 The Great War as seen by George Grosz, 1917

great effects on men's minds. European civilization is whatever most Europeans, as citizens, were doing at the time. In the period covered by this book, they were either making war or encountering economic problems. Therefore war and economics make up their civilization. I think that many of the things which civilized people did were highly barbarous, but this is a personal whim which I have tried to keep out of the text.

A.J.P.T.

In 1914 Europe was a single civilized community, more so even than at the height of the Roman Empire. A man could travel across the length and breadth of the Continent without a passport until he reached the frontiers of Russia and the Ottoman empire. He could settle in a foreign country for work or leisure without legal formalities except, occasionally, some health requirements. Every currency was as good as gold, though this security rested ultimately on the skill of financiers in the City of London. There were common political forms. Though there were only two republics in Europe (France and Portugal – Switzerland was technically a confederation, not a republic), every state except Monaco possessed some form of constitution limiting the power of the monarch to a greater or lesser degree. Nearly everywhere men could be sure of reasonably fair treatment in the courts of law. No one was killed for religious reasons. No one was killed for political reasons, despite the somewhat synthetic bitterness often shown in political disputes. Private property was everywhere secure, and in nearly all countries something was done to temper the extreme rigours of poverty.

Civilization was predominantly urban, and the towns all had much the same character. The three great symbols of modern architecture were the railway station, the town hall and, on the Continent of Europe, the opera house. Trains ran across the Continent with only a short stop at frontiers, overcoming even the obstacle of the broad gauge in Russia and Spain. Every town provided the same services – water, gas, electricity, and especially electric trams. Every opera house performed much the same repertory. Citizens of every country and of every class dressed much alike – national costume was worn only by peasants or as fancy dress. All European citizens took much the same meals at much the same times, except that the Russians ate their dinner at three o'clock and most English people at midday, not

2 Milan railway station

3 Paris *Opéra*

4 Stockholm Town Hall

German territory in 1914

Austria-Hungary in 1914

Russian territory lost after the v

GREAT BRITAIN

IRISH FREE STATE

Dublin

Londo

Pa

FRA

PORTUGAL

Lisbon

Madrid

SPAIN

5. Europe before and after the First World War

in the evening. All Europeans had much the same beliefs. All were Christians except in Turkey. Even the division into three cults – Roman Catholic, Orthodox, and Protestant – was less important than their common outlook in morality and philosophy, vaguely Christian and, a good deal more emphatically, optimistically liberal. All, despite racial differences, looked much alike. All were pink or, as it is absurdly called, 'white' in colour.

Europe dominated the world. Three European powers – France, Great Britain, and Russia – controlled 80 per cent of the world's surface. Three European powers – France, Germany, and Great Britain – had over half the world's industry and half its international trade. Siam was the only country in the world which escaped domination by Europeans at one time or another. Nor did any non-European country yet appear as a rival. On the contrary, everyone outside Europe tried to turn himself into a European as quickly as he could – in appearance, in outlook, above all in industrialization. By 1914 only two countries had succeeded. Japan seemed outwardly to be an industrial country of European type. The United States were already the greatest single industrial power in the world. But the Americans, apart from the Negroes and a handful of Red Indians, were Europeans in origin and character. In any case, the United States were still turned in on themselves. American goods had made little impact on the European market, nor was America yet a formidable competitor in the markets of the world. Indeed, the United States were still a debtor country, largely financed by the City of London like any colonial area.

The happy unity of Europe was threatened by some great divisions. The first and seemingly the most important was class. The propertied classes had, on the whole, made up their quarrels, despite continuing differences and conflicts between the landed aristocracy and the urban capitalists or *bourgeoisie*. Peasants still resented their landlords, particularly where this resentment was reinforced by national feelings, as it was in Ireland, Poland, and much of Austria-Hungary. But the peasants were no longer tied to the soil. They could escape their class war by leaving the land and going to the nearest town or to the United States. Little danger remained of a *Jacquerie*. Class conflict

6 The last emperor. George V as Emperor of India at Delhi in 1911

7 Keir Hardie, British Socialist, addresses a rally in Trafalgar Square, 1913

between industrial workers and their employers seemed a greater threat. The workers were becoming increasingly class-conscious, were increasingly demanding a greater share of the national wealth. There were Socialist parties in every country, usually represented in parliament. Yet even this class conflict was taking on civilized forms. Trade unions had a legal existence nearly everywhere, and usually some real power. The Socialist parties had become reformist in spirit, if not in phrase. They were part of the political system, often on the point of supporting governments or even forming them. A few Russian exiles still dreamt of 'revolution'. The chairman of the Socialist International, Vandervelde, himself a minister in Belgium, let them talk on. Lenin and Trotsky, he said, were not men of action.

The other division was national or, what was not quite the same thing, the division into sovereign states. Most of the national conflicts indeed were within states, particularly within Austria-Hungary and what remained of the Ottoman empire. The states themselves had few conflicts of a national kind across their frontiers. The French resented the loss of Alsace and Lorraine, though less bitterly than forty years before. The Italians, or some of them, clamoured for Trieste and South Tyrol. But many qualified judges were confident that the frontiers of Europe were fixed for good. They expected conflict, if any came, over the spoils of the rest of the world – a battle for empire. What they did not foresee was that those great machines of power, the armed forces, might lurch into conflict of themselves and drag the peoples of Europe after them. The European states performed many peaceful functions: they maintained law and order, gave security to individuals and to property, and promoted welfare. But their greatest task – that of the Great Powers, at any rate – was to maintain power for external purposes. The Continental Great Powers all operated universal military service, France and Germany completely, the other three – Austria-Hungary, Italy, and Russia – more theoretically. Great Britain had only a volunteer army and relied for security mainly on her navy – the largest fleet in the world.

There had been no war between European Great Powers since 1871, though there had been many alarms. Peace had been maintained by accident or by the working of some unseen natural law. There was little machinery for settling international disputes or preventing war, other than the usual diplomatic relations between

8 Royal meeting. Kaiser Wilhelm greets the King of Italy in Venice

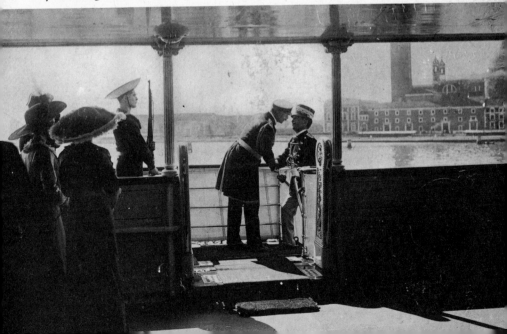

sovereign states. Peace rested, in fact, on the assumption that, in any dispute, one power or group of powers would give way rather than run the risk of war. Armaments were fondly regarded as a 'deterrent', and men said confidently: 'If you want peace, prepare for war.' Was there some change of spirit in 1914 which made this confidence less justified? Some historians say so. They assert that tension between the Great Powers was mounting and that each conflict was more difficult to settle by compromise. There is a good deal to be said on the other side, and maybe the tensions of 1914 seem greater only because they ended in war. Some of the Great Powers were on rather better terms than they had been a few years before. In particular, the three most advanced powers – France, Germany, and Great Britain – showed signs of drawing together at the expense of the two east European empires, Russia and Austria-Hungary. Both France and Great Britain had agreed to co-operate with Germany over the Baghdad railway. Great Britain and Germany contemplated a partition of the Portuguese colonies. Some highly placed Germans wanted to jettison their alliance with Austria-Hungary, while French politicians of the Left were equally cool towards Russia.

9 An offensive that failed.
Militant suffragettes being
escorted through St James's Park
after an unsuccessful attack
on Buckingham Palace in May 1914

Perhaps war was becoming more likely in a vaguer, emotional way. Violence was penetrating political life. Rebellion threatened in Ulster. Suffragettes practised direct action throughout Great Britain. Industrial disputes provoked armed conflict in Russia and Italy. The Austrian parliament had been suspended as unmanageable. Most curiously, the traditional standards of art and culture were being broken down, as if artists unconsciously anticipated the destruction of the Great War. A new art gallery in Vienna, named Sezession, symbolized this spirit of revolt. The Futurists were knocking the sense out of poetry. The Cubists were creating abstract, geometrical forms, thus ending a tradition of representational art which had dominated Europe for five hundred years. The Cubist movement drew on nearly all European countries and counted Russians, Poles, Germans, Spaniards among its principal exponents. In music, Schoenberg, Berg, and Webern sounded a discordant note against the diatonic scale. In 1913, Stravinsky's *Rite of Spring* provoked days of rioting in Paris. Previously artists had been Bohemians; now they were rebels, proudly displaying their hostility to society. Men's nerves were on edge – or so we surmise in retrospect.

17

10, 11, 12 Above, *Young Girl with Guitar,* painted in 1913 by Braque, one of the leading Cubists. Léger's *City* (opposite above) was painted in 1919. When Kokoschka's *The Tempest* (right) was exhibited at the Sezession in Vienna in 1914 it aroused violent reactions

However, war did not come in 1914 from the welling up of deep, uncontrollable forces. It occurred as the result of premeditated and, in a sense, rational acts. The statesmen decided, and the peoples applauded. The assassination of Archduke Franz Ferdinand at Sarajevo by South Slav nationalists on 28 June was an occasion, not a cause, and it would have been recognized at once as an operation in Serb politics if it had not become entangled with the European war. Nor was there anything outrageously exceptional in the Austro-Hungarian demands on Serbia. It was an accepted convention of the time that great powers bullied small ones. The new factor was the resolve of Germany's rulers to bully great powers also. Kaiser William II and Bethmann Hollweg, his Chancellor, seem at first to have made this resolve without a clear idea of what they were doing. Later they stuck to it in helpless obstinacy.

13 Appointment with an assassin. Archduke Franz Ferdinand and his wife set out for a drive in Sarajevo on 28 June 1914

Did Germany's rulers deliberately launch a European war, either from apprehension or to establish their domination over the Continent? The answers by historians have gone up and down with the years. Immediately after the outbreak of war, *Entente* historians usually declared that Germany had followed a course of planned aggression, while German historians claimed that she had acted in self-defence. Between the wars, most historians came to agree that the war had started by mistake. Now we seem back at the view that German militarism was mainly responsible. Germany was the greatest power in Europe -- the strongest economically, and apparently the one with the greatest future. Her outward equality with the other Continental powers did not correspond with her real preponderance compared to them. Moreover, the German military carried greater weight in society and in politics than they did elsewhere. It was easy

14, 15 Recruits for war in Germany and England

16 The famous recruiting poster, using Kitchener's likeness

for Germany's rulers to slip into believing that they both could and should lay down the law to others. Besides, they had to do so. All the Great Powers had elaborate plans for mobilizing their vast armies. Only the Germans merged these into plans for actual war. The others could mobilize and stand still; Germany could not. The German generals and statesmen were prisoners of the railway-timetables which they had worked out in the previous years. Technically the war started because the Germans wanted to get their blow in first. Men had, of course, debated everywhere what their country could gain if war came, and perhaps the Germans had debated a bit more than others. But in August 1914 the aim of the Germans and of

22

17 Official wartime art. *The Harvest of Battle*, painted in 1919 by C.R.W. Nevinson

everyone else was victory for its own sake. The war aims were worked out only after fighting had started.

The war was an affair of the Great Powers. All of them except Italy were in it from the start. Serbia and Belgium were the only small countries involved, and neither represented a prize of war in itself, though perhaps some Austrians thought otherwise about Serbia. The war was not a war for practical prizes; it was a true struggle for mastery. All the generals fought for victory. All the peoples fought for defence, or so they imagined. There was universal enthusiasm for war to the astonishment, or disappointment, of those who had expected war to be answered by social revolution. The

23

18 German artillery troops on horseback passing through Brussels in 1914

Germans, including even the Social Democrats, were defending the Fatherland against barbarous and autocratic Russia. The Russians were defending Mother Russia against the Germans. The French were defending their national territory. The British, not directly menaced themselves, were fighting in defence of gallant little Belgium. Yet all believed that future security could be found only by defeating the enemy and crippling him permanently. Total victory was regarded as the only sure means of defence.

Most of the combatants believed also that they were fighting for some noble cause. The Allied Powers, opposed to Germany, had the easier task in infusing idealism into their war. Germany was technically the aggressor, and her attack on Belgium was, moreover, aggression of a peculiarly flagrant kind. Her conduct of war was also soon characterized as peculiarly brutal. War is never a pleasant operation, and the alleged German atrocities in Belgium were perhaps no worse than those in previous wars – certainly no worse than those committed by Europeans when conquering non-European peoples. But after forty years of European peace, they rang round the world, and the Germans were denounced as 'Huns', a name which their emperor, William II, had himself conveniently provided for them. On the whole, however, the rules of war were observed. The Red Cross was almost universally respected. No belligerent used dum-dum bullets. The worst breach of restrictions was poison gas, a practice which the Germans started and which all the others then adopted to the best of their ability. The British were the only ones deliberately to ill-treat prisoners of war, when they shackled captured U-boat crews, and they soon dropped this practice when the Germans threatened to retaliate. The British, too, did not adhere to their principle against the Boers of conducting an all-white war. They brought Indian troops to France, as the French brought coloured Africans, and would have brought more if the climate had not proved unfavourable.

19 Light railway transport for German troops heading towards the front

Still, by and large, the war between the fighting men was conducted according to what were regarded, strangely or not, as civilized principles. Greater bitterness came into the war when it affected civilians – partly because it affected them more than previous wars had done, more because civilians were now citizens who could voice their feelings and whose feelings mattered. The Germans alone had conquered populations on their hands -- Belgium and north-east France in the west, Russian Poland in the east, and, though they behaved no worse than the French had done under similar circumstances in Napoleon's time, they also behaved no better. Direct attacks on civilians were new. The German naval bombardments of Scarborough and West Hartlepool and the dropping of bombs on English towns from Zeppelins and aircraft, trivial though both were, caused more hysteria in England than the military massacres on the western front.

21 Protected by masks, German troops make an assault under support of a gas cloud

20 New methods of war.
Allied merchant vessels
being attacked
by a German submarine
in 1917

Worst of all was the mutual blockade. The British enforced a blockade of Germany by the distant unseen pressure of sea power and pleaded that, though they were indeed cutting off civilian supplies, they were doing it without actually killing civilian crews. The Germans had to rely on submarines or U-boats, and these could only operate successfully by sinking ships at sight – a practice which they finally adopted, with disastrous effect, in January 1917. Both sides accumulated moral grievances. The Germans accused the British of starving women and children. The British accused the Germans of murder on the high seas. Both accusations were justified. Both offences sprang from the fact that war was no longer confined to actual fighting, but was the act of whole nations. The change was condemned as uncivilized, a return to barbarism. Rather, it bore witness that in the new civilization all citizens were full members of the community – in this case a community at war.

The armies themselves were no longer professional forces, detached from the community. They were, in the French phrase, 'the nation in arms'. All the Continental Great Powers at once put armies of millions into the field and soon swelled the numbers by millions more. Great Britain relied on voluntary recruitment until 1916 and raised over three million men by this method – the greatest surge of willing patriotism ever recorded. By October 1914, the end of the fighting season, it was clear that the war had not produced decisive victory in either east or west and that it would go on for a long time. The millions of soldiers were withdrawn indefinitely from civilian life. Industry and agriculture had to make do with fewer workers or to train new ones. The state cared for soldiers' wives and children – a thing it had not done in previous wars. Civilian life had to be carried on without the fighting men. Moreover, this life itself changed its character. The armies had set out fully equipped, and men at first assumed that this initial equipment would carry them through to victory. Now new equipment had to be ceaselessly provided on an ever-increasing scale. The first call for 'Business as usual' was silenced. Labour and capital were diverted from their normal activities to the production of munitions.

The existing social and economic order could not fulfil this requirement. It rested on the assumption that the needs of society would be met if every man pursued his own advantage. In wartime this assumption did not work, though many men, soon to be branded as profiteers, still acted on it. At first the makers of war relied on patriotic enthusiasm. They did not know anything else to rely on and, besides, the enthusiasm was there. War always evokes loyalty. It also evokes hatred. A century before, English children had been told that Napoleon would eat them if they misbehaved. Now the need for passion was greater: men everywhere had to be convinced that something more was at stake than mere victory over some other Great Power. The British and French peoples, though in alliance with autocratic Russia, were told that they were fighting for democracy and freedom. The Germans answered by boasting the superiority of their 'culture' over the decadent civilization of the west. There was something real in this clash of phrases. The British

22, 23 The Press Lord and the Profiteer. Lord Northcliffe, in the centre, visits the Italian front in 1916; right, a typical drawing by Grosz

and French were essentially on the defensive; they were seeking to maintain the old Europe of sovereign states and, less sincerely, of individual freedom. The Germans were groping towards a more or less united Europe, run of course by themselves and for their benefit, but a planned repudiation of international anarchy all the same. A German Social Democrat exclaimed, not untruly, in 1915, when he looked at Germany's conquests: 'Socialism as far as the eye can see.' This German socialism was not attractive to others.

Not only was passion needed for war. The instrument of passion was there. The peoples of Europe were predominantly literate, thanks to elementary education, though less so in eastern Europe than in the west. Newspapers were now read by the masses, not by a select few, and the appetite for war news – not least for the casualty lists – pushed circulations still higher. Newspaper proprietors, of whom Lord Northcliffe was the most famous, sought to direct both the politics and strategy of war. Many a fierce combatant occupied

24 Racialism in action. A crowd in the East End of London threaten a German butcher-shop in June 1915

an editorial chair and daily killed the enemy with his pen. Writers and academics mobilized their intellectual abilities. Thomas Mann demonstrated the superiority of German culture. H.G. Wells discovered that this was a war to end war. Historians proved, to their own satisfaction, the war-guilt of the enemy and the innocence of their own country. Poets composed hymns of hate. In Germany 1,347 intellectuals put their names to an annexationist programme, and the academics of other countries, though less disciplined, were equally busy. The public responded to these drums of war. When all else failed, they sacked the shops of bakers with foreign names and detected a spy in any suspicious stranger.

The political leaders added to the clamour, defining – or obscuring – the war aims of their countries in a cloud of words. It did not occur to them that there was anything else they could do. They had provided the armies; now they stood aside while the generals won the war for them. The French government virtually abdicated in favour of Joffre, the commander-in-chief. The Chancellor of Germany regarded himself as the servant of the High Command.

In Great Britain Lord Kitchener, conqueror of the Sudan and of the Boers, became Secretary for War and ran the war almost single-handed. Only generals, it was felt, understood the art of war. Yet none of the generals except the British had any experience of war, and the British experiences against the Boers provided few useful lessons for the western front. The generals had acquired one skill only during the long years of peace: they knew how to move large numbers of men and horses by train. Once the men arrived at the railhead, their bodies were flung against the enemy in a tactic which had not changed since Napoleonic, or even Roman, times.

Army officers in every country came from the conservative privi-leged classes and had no contact with the scientific creative spirit of the age. When their first brutal onslaughts failed, they cried out for more men or, at most, for more shells. They did not cry out for new methods. No general consulted a civil engineer or the head of a great industrial concern, and the only general with a scientific training, the Australian, Sir John Monash, remained in a subordinate position until the end of the war. The generals had little interest in new weapons. They had accepted the rifle, though mainly in order to stick a bayonet on the end of it – a variant of the pike. They resented the machine-gun as a defensive and therefore cowardly weapon. They regarded the tank and aeroplane with suspicion. They were even indifferent to motor transport for their men, though not for themselves. They sat in remote headquarters, working on railway-timetables and accumulating an ever greater weight of men and shells.

Weight was the only offensive idea in the first two years of the war – the only idea of Joffre and of Haig, who became British commander-in-chief in the autumn of 1915, and the only idea of Hindenburg and Ludendorff on the eastern front. All acquired great public reputation from a record of failure. Machine-guns were effec-tive in stopping men. Earth, thrown up by the spade, was effective in stopping shells. Even if the occasional dent or gap were made, it could be closed by new defenders, who arrived by rail more rapidly than the attackers could plod forward on foot. Joffre's offensive in Champagne in 1915 and Haig's offensive on the Somme in 1916 hardly moved their respective lines forward at all. The Germans

25, 26 The Allied war lords. George V meets with General Joffre, President Poincaré, General Foch and Sir Douglas Haig at Beauquesne, France. Right, Lord Kitchener leaving the War Office

achieved a real breakthrough on the eastern front at Gorlice in May 1915 and were then defeated by their own weight; they could not move across the wastes of Russian Poland fast enough to prevent the Russians from forming a new defensive line. Verdun was the crowning symbol of this war. Its loss would have been no strategic disaster for the French; its capture would have brought no strategic gain for the Germans. Yet both sides sent soldiers through this mincing-machine by the hundred thousand, merely in order to batter against each other. Joffre openly announced that the war could be won only by attrition, even if it meant killing three French and British for every two German soldiers. Sir William Robertson, Chief of the Imperial General Staff, approved and called this the principle of the longer purse.

By 1916 the glory and romance had gone out of war – a profound change in men's outlook. Previously, war and civilization had not been regarded as incompatible. On the contrary, success in war was seen as evidence of superior civilization. The victories of the imperial legions proved the merits of Roman civilization, just as the victories of Napoleon demonstrated those of French revolutionary ideas. The almost unbroken run of European victories over Asiatics and Africans in the nineteenth century showed that Europe possessed the most advanced civilization in the world. Gladstone, though hardly a man of war, had the bells rung for Wolseley's victory over the Egyptians at Tel-el-Kebir and declared: 'This is a great day for civilization.' European civilization advanced across the world with the cheerful slogan: 'We have the Maxim gun, and they have not.' When the Japanese defeated the Russians in 1905, some men felt that European civilization was in decline, but most were glad to welcome Japan into the company of the civilized European powers. The mutual slaughter between 1914 and 1916 shook the happy equation between civilization and victory. Most of the civilized powers were at war. Yet none had won or was in sight of victory. Instead, war threatened to destroy the moral and material achievements of civilization.

27 The German war lords. The Kaiser confers with Field-Marshal Hindenburg and General Ludendorff

There were two possible and conflicting answers to this threat. One was to wage war more fiercely than ever. If the more civilized power was the one which won, as by previous definition it had been, then the belligerents should develop the resources of civilization for war purposes: more skill, more science, more effective political and economic organization. The other answer was to end the war either by appealing to the standards of the existing civilization or by repudiating them in the name of a new one. Both answers were explored in the hard winter of 1916 to 1917 – a period which was much more a turning-point in the history of civilization than the outbreak of war in August 1914 had been. The call for a fiercer war brought new men to power, though not all men of the same type. In France and Great Britain, civilian politicians triumphed over the military leaders to a greater or lesser degree. In December 1916, Lloyd George overthrew Asquith and established his authority over

28 Looking for the Hindenburg line. British troops pursue the retreating Germans across the Somme in 1917

29 Verdun. The fortress of Vaux in 1916 just before the successful German attack ▶

30, 31 The national heroes. Clemenceau and Lloyd George

the admirals, though not until late in the day over the generals. In France, Joffre was discarded; no subsequent commander quite enjoyed his prestige or his power; and in November 1917, Clemenceau became virtual dictator over generals and parliament alike. Even the Russian revolution of March 1917 was at first used to substitute more energetic and more warlike politicians for the feeble Tsar. In Germany, on the other hand, Hindenburg and Ludendorff, now at the High Command, secured the dismissal of Bethmann Hollweg, the Chancellor, and became the real wielders of political power.

This was not merely a change of men; it was also the triumph of new methods. The nations of Europe had at first tried to run the war as a luxury – an extra which did not interfere with the ordinary rules of social and economic life. Now they all adopted war socialism. Rationing took the place of the free market; direction of capital and of labour superseded free enterprise; the economic life of every nation was planned from above. There was a levelling of classes, though more in theory than in practice. There was also a levelling of the sexes. Women had long agitated for their emancipation; now they were emancipated, thanks to the needs of war and not from any moral principle. Women worked in factories and in offices. They drove trams and buses. They became wage-earners, like men. A rigid

English Conservative announced: 'It must be recognized that women's place is no longer in the home' – a sentence of death for the old masculine outlook. Men's thoughts also were planned. Active propaganda took the place of negative censorship: propaganda to strengthen the fighting spirit at home and also, less successfully, to shake that of the enemy. Statesmen were somewhat ashamed of their invention and described propaganda as 'information' when they acknowledged it at all. But there was no escape. Most adults had become servants of the state. In return, the state had to tell them what to think as well as what to do.

The new methods were not strikingly efficient. Controls and economic direction were improvised in response to immediate alarms, not as part of any general policy. Thus food rationing was introduced in Great Britain one week-end to get rid of queues at butchers' shops. The planners had no reliable statistics and rarely knew what the results of their plans would be. Every army, for instance, had lamented the shortage of shells. In response the planners acted so effectively that before the end of the war every army,

32 Emancipated Englishwomen. Munitions workers at Woolwich Arsenal

including even the Russian, had more shells than it could use. The governments poured out vast sums of money and made little or no effort to balance their accounts. There was no increase of taxation in either France or Germany. Even in Great Britain taxes met less than a third of the war's cost. The war was paid for by borrowing, with a promise that the defeated enemy would pay afterwards. Loans were raised with a rattle of public enthusiasm, especially in Germany where lenders were allowed to drive nails into a wooden statue of Hindenburg – a strange, pagan ritual. War brought hardship to the poor and made the rich richer. Social resentment mounted. The profiteer in his top hat became as much a symbol of the war as the begrimed ordinary soldier in the trenches. As the patriotic spirit of the early days weakened, the masses began to think that this was a war of the bosses, in which they were being slaughtered by an international combine of armament manufacturers.

Nevertheless, the discontent was on a surprisingly small scale. The strikes in the munition works, common in 1917, were dispelled by improved wages and working conditions. The representatives of the working classes were given some say in public affairs. In Great Britain a Labour leader – first Arthur Henderson, then George Barnes – sat in the War Cabinet. There were Socialist ministers in France. The German general, Groener, established a close partnership with the trade unions. Most surprising of all, the discontent rarely lapped over to the armed forces. Czechs and Poles deserted from the Austro-Hungarian army, but their desertion was due to national feeling, not to dislike of fighting, as they showed by forming Polish and Czech legions on the Allied side. There were mutinies during 1917 in both the German and Austro-Hungarian navies, but in resentment against inaction, not against active service. The Russian revolution of 1917 is sometimes attributed to discontent in the army, but this was not so. The revolution started among the civilians and reservists in Petrograd, and the army joined in only when the revolution had succeeded. One army was devastated by mutiny – a unique case. After the disastrous offensive launched by Nivelle in April 1917, the French troops could stand no more. Fifty-four divisions refused to obey orders, and some even talked of marching on Paris, though

33 The wooden titan. This colossal statue of Hindenburg was unveiled in Berlin in September 1915 as part of a fund-raising campaign

they did not do so. Pétain, the new commander-in-chief, restored discipline by promising that there would be no more wild offensives, and within a few months the French army was again an effective fighting force.

The war demonstrated anew the almost endless patience of ordinary men. Opposition to the war, or attempts to end it, came only from the educated minority – leaders without an army. This opposition was almost entirely secular. The ministers of the Christian religion were busy preaching patriotic sermons and blessing the weapons of war. The Protestant and Orthodox churches had no difficulty in associating closely with the state. Roman Catholicism was more international, and in 1917 Pope Benedict XV made a cautious effort to mediate between the combatants. He was rebuffed by the great Allies, none of whom was officially a Roman Catholic country. In any case, the papacy was in a conservative mood after Leo XIII's attempt at modernization, and Benedict XV seemed more

34, 35, 36 Voices against war. Siegfried Sassoon, Henri Barbusse, Romain Rolland

concerned to preserve Austria-Hungary, the one impeccably conservative power, than to bring the war to an end. Apart from this isolated episode, only the Society of Friends (Quakers) bore witness to the gospel of the Prince of Peace.

This gospel was served more widely by non-believers: the heirs of Voltaire and the nineteenth-century rationalists, men who aspired to remain sane in a world gone mad. Their weapon was cool argument: pamphlets with a small circulation, addresses to the devoted few at meetings which were often broken up by soldiers on leave. In 1916 they were reinforced by English poets, Sassoon in particular, and in France by novelists. *Le Feu*, by Henri Barbusse, was the first literary protest against modern war and set the pattern for all later books on this theme. Romain Rolland acted from Switzerland as a sort of secular pope to the opponents of war. Not all these men were Socialists or even men of the Left. Lord Lansdowne, who advocated a compromise peace in England, was a high aristocrat and extreme Conservative. Caillaux, the leader of the peace party in France, though a Radical, spoke for financiers and bankers. Still, these were exceptions. The call for reason and moderation came mainly from Socialists: Ramsay MacDonald in Great Britain, Karl Kautsky and Karl Liebknecht in Germany, Fritz Adler in Austria. Their Marxism, even if they held it, was subordinated to their humanity. They held that the war was a destructive folly, and hoped to end it by general conciliation. In practice, their campaign was directed against the political leaders in each country, and they tended to suggest that the masses were saner and more pacific than their rulers – a suggestion not much supported by facts.

Ironically, the advocates of a sane peace found one ally among the statesmen: Woodrow Wilson, President of the United States. Wilson, too, was a rational idealist, convinced of his own moral and intellectual superiority. He, too, wanted Peace without Victory and believed that the United States should remain neutral in order to mediate between the belligerent powers, or perhaps even to impose peace on them. Many Americans shared Wilson's outlook. They felt morally superior to the old decadent Europe which they or their ancestors had left, and acknowledged at most a mission to rescue Europe from its follies. The automobile manufacturer, Henry Ford, commissioned a Peace Ship which cruised, pathetic and disregarded, in European waters. Wilson's own disquisitions on peace were no more effective.

37 A pacifist meeting in London in 1917

There was equivocation in the attitude of many Americans, including Wilson himself. Mostly Anglo-Saxon in origin, they could not escape some sympathy with Great Britain, however much they proclaimed neutrality. Moreover, there was a practical stake. American industry boomed, supplying the belligerents with food and raw materials. Thanks to the effectiveness of the British blockade, this meant in practice supplying Great Britain and France. The Germans retaliated with submarine warfare, whereupon Wilson asserted the freedom of the seas. In January 1917, the Germans took off all restrictions on their submarines. Wilson, after some hesitation, declared war. It was ironical that he abandoned neutrality just when his mediation might have achieved some purpose at last. The summer of 1917 saw the only real gropings in Europe towards peace by negotiation. The provisional Russian government wanted to negotiate; the German Reichstag passed a peace resolution; Emperor Charles of Austria-Hungary actually negotiated. Though Wilson was no longer available as mediator, he still claimed to be above the battle, in spite of the United States's commitment to battle on the Allied side. Wilson was conducting a crusade, not engaging in a struggle for power. Since he could hardly crusade against both sides at once, he proposed to defeat Germany first and then impose his ideals on the Allies afterwards. The United States never became an Ally. They remained an Associated Power, an indication of the in-and-out position which they were to adopt towards Europe for the next fifty years.

The entry of the United States into the European war opened a new era in European civilization. In a long distant past, that civilization had been shaped, and sometimes ruined, by impacts from outside, particularly by the barbarian invasions. Ever since the Turks had been halted at the gates of Vienna more than two hundred years before, the traffic between Europe and the rest of the world had been all one way. Europeans were everywhere the invaders and conquerors. They spread over the world, subdued and exploited it. Now the New World bounced back. Henceforth, European affairs were to be influenced, sometimes to be shaped, from outside. The Americans were Europeans with a difference: Europeans in origin and largely in culture, but without the Europeans' traditions of political behaviour. Some Americans cared for their nations of origin – Irish, Czech, or Polish – and joined with Wilson in advocating national self-determination. Very few cared for the European welter of sovereign states. They disliked the European monarchies and, still more, the extension of European empires overseas. They wanted all Europeans to become peaceful, prosperous, and sensible, like themselves. They could not understand why Europeans failed to abandon their parochial loyalties. European civilization, once apparently so superior and complacent, was now under challenge. Thus questioned by the Americans, Europeans began to doubt themselves. Morally, their age of supremacy was over.

In practical terms, America's declaration of war had a quite different effect: it ensured the victory of one group of European powers over the other. By 1917 Germany had defeated Russia and seemed near to defeating France. Great Britain on her own had not much chance of defeating Germany, whatever Lloyd George might say about the knock-out blow. British and French statesmen dickered gloomily with the idea of peace negotiations; once America was in the war, they could throw such ideas aside. Total victory was possible after all. Yet it was victory with a difference. Wilson was fighting for great principles, not for national security. After all, no one could possibly imagine that the United States were threatened by Germany, as Great Britain and France alleged that they were. The Allies, too, had to parade their great principles, in order to satisfy their new associate. The parade was not merely for show. The peoples, perhaps even the governments, believed that they were fighting a war of ideals, not a war of power. Still, the belief would not have been so strong, or the principles so ringingly asserted, had it not been for the participation of the United States.

Wilson's new position as a maker of war had an immediate impact on the men of moderation and sanity. After all, he was one of themselves. His principles were their principles. Like them, he had insisted that force settled nothing; like them, he had claimed that reason and conciliation were the only effective instruments of international relations. Now this same Wilson was preaching force – 'force to the

43

uttermost'. He had become the foremost advocate of total victory and no compromise. The men of moderation and sanity were caught by Wilson. They had invested their moral capital in him and could not now sell out. They had condemned war for mundane objects, and now endorsed it for celestial ones. The war became 'a war to end war'. And if that were not achieved, there would have to be still more wars for the same purpose – holy wars, wars of principle, not wars of interest. Wilson's position already foreshadowed the inter-wars bewilderment of the League of Nations: an organization for preventing war, which could operate ultimately only by itself con-ducting war. In April 1917 civilized man began the pursuit of a strange mirage: perpetual war for the sake of perpetual peace.

Wilson was the apostle of a new age. A rival apostle appeared on the stage at almost exactly the same time. In 1915 and 1916, when a few high-minded Socialists had gathered in Switzerland and issued rational appeals against the war, one man told them harshly that they were wasting their time. War, he declared, was not an accident or a foolish mistake. It was the inevitable result of contemporary civilization – 'capitalism', to give it an economic name. Appeals to reason would achieve nothing. The war could be ended only by destroying the existing social order and creating a new one. 'End the war' and 'No more war' were futile slogans. The only solution was: 'Turn the imperialist war into a civil war.'

Most Socialists disregarded this solitary, implacable voice. It was the voice of Lenin, then an exile in Switzerland, leader of an almost non-existent Russian party. Lenin himself did not expect to have much effect. Early in 1917 he told a group of Swiss students: 'We older men will not live to see the Socialist revolution.' Then, with startling suddenness, his chance came. In March 1917 there were food riots in Petrograd, which turned into demands for the overthrow of the Tsar. Upon the abdication of Tsar Nicholas II, Russia became a democratic republic, of course only in theory. No parliamentary elections were held, and the provisional government was composed of any Liberal or Socialist politicians who happened to be available. Lenin was able to return to Russia from Switzerland – strangely enough, with the approval of the German High Command, who rightly saw in him a troublemaker, though they did not foresee that he would make trouble for them as well as for others.

This first Russian revolution was not made directly against the war. Indeed, it was hoped by many that revolution would make Russia a more effective fighting power, as the Jacobin revolution had done for France in 1793. When Lenin arrived in Petrograd, he found that he was almost alone in wanting a further revolution. Even his own followers were shocked by his extreme views, but Lenin was not dismayed. He too, like Wilson, was convinced of his own intellectual superiority and righteousness. Many later writers have regarded Lenin as essentially Russian – almost a barbarian in European eyes – and have presented his policy as a Russian repudiation of Europe. This is a grave misunderstanding. The basic elements in Lenin were Marxist, not Russian. His master, Karl Marx, was a learned German from the Rhineland, who spent most of his working life in the British Museum. Lenin regarded himself as an international Socialist, and his aim was to start a revolution which would sweep across Europe, not to pull Russia out of Europe. His ideas belonged to the traditions of European Socialism: hostility to the governing classes; reliance on the wisdom and virtue of the industrial workers; and conviction that Socialism would end all earthly evils. For Lenin, Utopia was just round the corner: this was the great difference between him and most other Socialists. They doubted whether Socialism could be established and, still more, whether they could establish it. Lenin had no doubts. He had only to seize power, and all problems would be solved. This was not far removed from Wilson's belief that all would be well, once he controlled the destinies of the world.

Thus European affairs, during 1917, moved on two planes. On the practical plane of war, the German armies successfully battered the Russians into defeat. The British armies tried to do the same with the Germans in the mud of Flanders and failed. The war ate up more men and more materials. Civilian life was increasingly controlled and degraded. Meanwhile, the two Utopians, Wilson and Lenin, prepared to supersede the old order. American armies were assembled and trained. Wilson formulated idealistic terms of peace, to be imposed on enemies and Allies alike when the war was won. Lenin continued to call for a further revolution. The more active among the war-weary peoples of Russia listened to him, while the routine politicians of the provisional government found power slipping from their hands. In November Lenin's party, the Bolsheviks, seized power in an almost bloodless revolution. They claimed to rule in the name of the Soviets – councils of delegates from factories and fighting units which had sprung up after the first revolution. Many of these delegates were indeed Bolsheviks or, to give them the new name which Lenin promulgated shortly afterwards, Communists. Still, these delegates, Communist or not, had little choice. Lenin and his associates simply informed them that they had chosen Lenin and his associates as the government of People's Commissars. New equations were established almost without argument. The rule of the working class or proletariat was true democracy. The Soviets expressed the will of the working class. The Communist party expressed the will of the Soviets. Lenin expressed the will of the Communist party. Therefore Lenin's dictatorship was the high point of democracy.

It is idle to speculate on the correctness of these propositions. Whether true or false, Lenin and most other Communists believed them; hence the confusions of Soviet affairs in later years. Lenin believed still more strongly in the certainty of his own success. He had seized power with two objects: one, immediate, to end the war throughout Europe; the other, slightly more remote, to establish Socialism all over the world. The Russian revolution was to be the first spark of a universal explosion. It never occurred to Lenin that it would remain an isolated event. His first act was the Decree on Peace: an announcement that the war was over so far as Russia was concerned, and an appeal that the workers in other countries should follow Russia's example. At the same time, Lenin decreed Socialism for all Russian industry – a more or less casual operation, as he supposed. Yet, at the very moment of creating a new social order, Lenin also revived or preserved an old one. He recognized, in an early flash of realism, that the so-called workers' revolution had to be tolerated by the peasant masses, and he therefore authorized the peasants to seize the land for themselves. Urban socialism, so far as

38, 39 The Bolshevik view of war. The Tsar, the Church and the rich man are carried by the suffering masses. Right, the tired Russian soldier

it existed, became an island in a sea of obscurantist individual proprietors.

The Bolshevik revolution had great effects in Europe, though hardly those Lenin had expected. The appeal to follow Russia's example did not succeed. Though there were strikes in Germany and in Austria-Hungary, these were against hard conditions, not against the war, and they ended when food rations were improved. The governing classes, not the masses, heard Lenin's appeal. Throughout the war they had contemplated with anxiety the moment when the peoples might lose the will to obey. Now they could identify war-weariness with Bolshevism, an alien conspiracy to destroy civilization. They used anti-Bolshevism as a shot in the arm for their war spirit. Victory, they believed, was the best remedy against Bolshevism, and they turned against Bolshevism the more fiercely because it stood in the way of victory. The German High Command wasted no time

47

in trying to conciliate the new rulers. They imposed a heavy indemnity and took from Russia a third of her European territory. Most prominent Bolsheviks were ashamed to contemplate peace with capitalist Germany, particularly on such terms, and wished to rattle the sabre of a revolutionary war.

The Allies did nothing to aid or encourage them. The British and French governments regarded the Bolshevik Decree on Peace as wilful treachery to civilization. They imagined that somewhere there was a deep fund of Russian strength and patriotism, and actually welcomed the harsh German conditions, believing that these would provoke both the overthrow of the Bolsheviks and a Russian renewal of the war. Lenin alone recognized the failure of his earlier hopes. Acknowledging that the European revolution, which he had counted on, had not happened, he argued that the Bolsheviks must buy time on terms, however harsh. The delay, he supposed, would be short; the Communists would soon resume their leadership of international revolution. Still, the delay was accepted. On 3 March 1918, Russia and Germany concluded the peace of Brest-Litovsk. This was Lenin's first compromise with reality, and it began the process which made Communism a Russian, not a world-wide, movement. A line was drawn between Russia and the rest of the civilized world. Each side blamed the other, the Allies complaining that Russia had withdrawn from European affairs, and Lenin and the Bolsheviks answering that Germany and the Allies had combined to exclude Russia.

The Allies soon gave Lenin further grounds for estrangement. They began military intervention in Russia, ostensibly to save her from the Germans, but with a hope also that the Bolsheviks might be toppled in the process. This step had great consequences, unforeseen at the time. The liberal powers of western Europe had debated for many years whether Germany or Russia represented the greater danger. The outbreak of war provided an answer. Germany became the enemy and Russia became the fighting Ally. Now the question was opened again. A few western statesmen, such as Lord Milner, wanted to reverse the answer: they favoured a compromise peace with Germany so that the civilized powers could unite against Bolshevism, both in Russia and at home. Most of the political leaders

40 Short-lived victory. Von Kühlmann, for Germany, signs the Treaty of Brest-Litovsk, while Count Czernin of Austria-Hungary looks on

failed to answer one way or the other. They took refuge in a vague hope that one day either Germany or Russia might become democratic and civilized, in their sense. Meanwhile the Allies had two wars on their hands instead of one and, still worse, the prospect of two rivals during an indefinite future.

In 1918 the danger from Bolshevism was fairly remote, that from the Germans very near. The German generals were no doubt the narrowest and most arrogant military caste in Europe, but, unlike other generals, they actually applied their minds to methods of making war. The result was not without paradox. Germany was the most highly industrialized state in Europe; yet the German armies achieved their great successes in the spring of 1918 by ingenuity, not by using machines. The limit of German military skill was to improve infantry tactics. It was the less imaginative British generals who developed the tank, or rather had its development thrust upon them. Tanks and, to a lesser extent, aeroplanes were a portent for the future. Until 1918, war – in the sense of actual combat – still turned

49

on human beings, and Ludendorff's last campaign was Napoleonic in its improvisations. With the advent of tanks, machines began to take the place of men, and war caught up with the mechanical spirit which characterized modern European civilization.

The last year of the war saw another innovation, though a temporary one. During the alarms of March 1918 the Allies achieved unity of command. Foch became Supreme Commander. Allied military and economic plans were co-ordinated. National sovereignty was eclipsed, but only for the duration of the war. International co-operation thus emerged as one of war's many evils. In any case, a greater Allied resource was the awareness that an American army was on its way to Europe. The United States forces did comparatively little fighting, and their total casualties were less than those of the Australians. The French and, even more, the British generals were anxious to win the war before the United States became the preponderant power; still, with the American armies at their back, they took risks which they would not have taken otherwise. Here, too, was a pattern for the future. Great Britain and France wanted to run the affairs of Europe without American interference and yet had a confidence, well placed or not, that the United States would come to their rescue if they made a mess of these affairs.

41 The supreme commander, General Foch

42 The weapon of the future. A British tank on the move

The war ended in a strangely contradictory way. In October the Germans appealed to President Wilson both for an armistice and for terms of peace. Wilson offered peace on the idealistic conditions which he had previously elaborated, known as the Fourteen Points. The German government accepted these conditions after some bargaining, and Wilson imposed the same conditions, with two reservations, on the Allies. As a further gesture to placate Wilson, the Germans transformed their country into a democratic, parliamentary state. The ideals championed by the revolutionaries of 1848 thus triumphed in Germany by American order. Wilson, however, referred the Germans to the military commanders for armistice conditions, and Foch dictated terms of Allied victory: the partial disarmament of Germany and an Allied occupation of the Rhineland.

Here were two conceptions of what the war had achieved. If Germany were sincere in accepting the Fourteen Points and adopting democracy, as Wilson held she was, there was no dividing line of principle between her and the Allies, and she could join the community of nations even sooner than France had done after the Napoleonic wars. But Foch, in the armistice terms, treated Germany as an irreconcilable, though defeated, enemy who must pay the penalty for losing a war. Both conceptions existed side by side. Both were operated, often confusingly by the same man. Which was the more decisive – that Wilson's ideals had triumphed or that the German armies had been defeated? The future was to show that the two conceptions cancelled out, and Europe got neither the blessings of a new order nor the restoration of the old one.

Germany's two allies, the Habsburg monarchy and the Ottoman empire, were brought down by her defeat, and indeed more catastrophically. Germany remained united and, however weakened, with all the resources of a Great Power, but the two empires fell to pieces. In 1914 there had been five emperors in Europe. By the end of 1918 there was one: the King of England, and he only as Emperor of India. The historical transformation went further. It needed a war fought in the twentieth century to liquidate the remains of ancient Rome. The Habsburgs had been for centuries Holy Roman Emperors and retained some shreds of Charlemagne's tradition. The Ottoman emperors had kept alive at Constantinople the spirit of Byzantium. Now both were gone. The link of continuity was snapped.

The fall of the dynasties shook also the classes which had been associated with them. The power of the landed aristocracy was broken in all the former Habsburg territories except Hungary, and the German capitalists of Vienna were equally weakened. The national states which took the place of the vanished Habsburg empire seemed a triumph for Wilson's principle of self-determination. But they also signified an assertion of traditions in a different form. Each separate nation had its history or invented one, and soon the new national states were advancing historical claims against each other much as the dynasts had done.

The end of the Ottoman empire caused less novelty so far as Europe was concerned. Most of Turkey's European lands had already been turned into national states before 1914. Constantinople remained in Turkish hands, after the failure of a Greek attempt to carry it off, but its place in the world was changed. The capital of Turkey was moved to Ankara in Asia Minor, and Constantinople, which had been, for a thousand years, the greatest city in Europe, dwindled into obscurity: a mere place with few memories and no importance. The Arab lands of the Ottoman empire were mostly shared out between France and Great Britain, who thus appeared, after all, to have been fighting the war for imperialist aims. There was one startling innovation. In November 1917 the British government announced that Palestine was to provide a national home for the Jews. Their immediate aim was to win Jewish support for the Allied cause and, rather more urgently, to devise an excuse for keeping the French at a safe distance from the Suez Canal. The British did not weigh seriously the effects of their promise. In particular, they did not contemplate how Jews could be settled in Palestine without disturbing the existing Arab population. The consequences were, however, remarkable. Though often persecuted, the Jews had been embedded for centuries past in the societies of many European countries and, despite their difference in religion and customs, sometimes as much at home there as any other inhabitants. Now the Jews were being invited to become an ordinary nation like the Irish or the Poles. Most of the Jews who returned to Palestine were Europeans in nearly everything, and their community became a piece of Europe inserted into Asia – a twentieth-century version of the Crusader states.

These were remote consequences of war, unforeseen on 11 November 1918 when the fighting ended on the western front. On that day men were conscious only of the destruction of war and rejoiced that it was over. On the Allied side, they rejoiced, too, at victory. But what did the victory mean? It brought security, at any rate for the short run, in the sense that no foreign conqueror occupied the national soil. Beyond that, the war seemed to have brought only devastation. Ten million Europeans had been killed. Many millions more were crippled. The accumulated wealth of centuries had been run down. Every belligerent country had vast internal debts, and every European Ally also had war-debts to the United States. The industrial system was dislocated by the demands of war. There were

43, 44, 45 Memorials of war in Paris (above left), London (below left) and Berlin (below)

46 The remnants of the Grande Place at Ypres

few compensations to show on the other side. The Allies had been fighting for great ideals, or so they claimed at Wilson's prodding. The ideals had substance: democracy, national self-determination, the sovereign rights of every independent state. These ideals did not flourish in wartime. Rather, they could take on life only as the memories of war faded.

Deepest of all, the Allies, and perhaps the Germans too, had been fighting against war itself – a war to end war. The phrase rang round the world. It was a contradiction. Only peace could end war, as the handful of sane men had insisted. The First World War was difficult to fit into the picture of a rational civilization advancing by ordered stages. The civilized men of the twentieth century had outdone in savagery the barbarians of all preceding ages, and their civilized virtues – organization, mechanical skill, self-sacrifice – had made war's savagery all the more terrible. Modern man had developed powers which he was not fit to use. European civilization had been weighed in the balance and found wanting.

The great men of the age – statesmen, writers, religious leaders – had claimed to be wiser and more humane than their predecessors. Yet nearly all of them embraced the passions of war, and the rest contemplated the storm with helpless resignation. The few who remained sane did little better. Their attempts at conciliation were narrowly rational. They tried to devise sensible terms for ending the war and failed to recognize that the warring powers wanted victory for its own sake, not for the prizes which it might bring. Lenin was the only man who did anything effective against the war, and his reward was to be shunned by the civilized community.

Nor were the masses more moderate or more generous than their rulers, whatever the enthusiasts for democracy might claim. Ordinary people were often war-weary, and the men in the trenches often expressed a rough lack of faith in their generals; but they went on with the war and joined in the outcry against those who tried to end it. Immediately after the war, there were free elections, based on universal suffrage, in nearly every European country. The victorious peoples, without exception, voted overwhelmingly for those who had conducted the war most fiercely, and even in defeated Germany the people did not give a clear majority to the Social Democrats, who had been at any rate less enthusiastic. The First World War, whatever its horrors, was a war which nearly everybody wanted, and wanted for its own sake. It is difficult to apply the word 'civilized' to a community which tolerated such events, yet twentieth-century Europeans still raised hands of complacent disapproval at the gladiatorial games of ancient Rome or at the human sacrifices of the Aztecs.

If the magnitude of an event be judged by the number of monuments to it, the Great War, as men called it, was the greatest event that ever happened. The Bolshevik rulers of Russia built no monuments to the war – a minor indication, though no doubt not deliberate, that they had repudiated the existing civilization. Elsewhere there were memorials in every town and village. They present a curious picture of popular taste, which has never been studied. The

simplest gave a long list of the dead, their names carved in stone. Most had some crudely naturalistic sculpture: an angel or a soldier, romantically upright, grasping a flag. None of them showed what the war was really like, though occasionally one was an actual instrument of destruction – a tank or a heavy gun. These monuments, by their very inadequacy, expressed men's bewilderment at the torments through which they had passed. The commemorations of the war showed the same bewilderment. They were held on 11 November, the day of the armistice, not on 28 June, the day when peace was signed. They celebrated the ending of the war, not victory, and expressed thankfulness that it was over, not rejoicing that anything substantial had been achieved. Memories bit deep – so deep that, even after the end of the Second World War, Remembrance Day was still in November, not in May. Men were still remembering the first war, not the second.

That first war seemed, perhaps was, more of a break in historical continuity, both as an end and a beginning. It came after a generation of European peace. Men did not know what to expect or, at any rate, the war turned out very differently from what they had expected. Their bewilderment had deeper causes. Many wars make sense, if the word can be used of such a senseless procedure. The great war which began at Valmy and ended at Waterloo (1792–1815) was predominantly a conflict between the traditional order and the revolution. The Second World War of the twentieth century was predominantly a war against National Socialism. But what was the First World War about? In essence it was a war against war, rather than a conflict of creeds. If victory had gone to the other side, the territorial arrangements would have been different. But would the character of the ensuing civilization have been much altered?

The shadow of the First World War hung over Europe for years afterwards. The war got the blame for everything which happened – for economic confusions, moral laxity, artistic innovations, and social unrest. Most of these things would no doubt have happened anyway, though perhaps not so quickly. The scars truly attributable to the war proved less deep than most people feared at the time. Despite the millions of war-dead, none of the leading combatants was pulled down from the ranks of the Great Powers as, say, Sweden and Holland had been in previous centuries. France came nearest to this, but her decline proved temporary. The material destruction was concentrated in a few areas – north-east France and the adjacent corner of Belgium suffering the most – and it was put right within a few years. Economists have calculated that the war retarded advance by about ten years. Most countries regained their pre-war level of industrial production in 1924 – Russia only in 1928 – and by 1929 had far surpassed it. The apparently crushing war-debts only transferred claims to wealth within the national communities, except, of course, for the debts to the United States, and these were paid only as long as American citizens lent European countries the money with which to pay them.

The damage of war was greater in men's minds, though this too was less than had been expected. Millions of men had been striving to kill each other. Yet only the defeated Germans, or some of them, took the habits of war back into civilian life. Elsewhere, the great majority of fighting men soon became civilians in thought and action, as though their war service had never been. At the end of the war, statesmen were apprehensive of 'Bolshevism' – meaning by this a collapse of the social order rather than a planned revolution. Little of their fears came true outside Russia. There was some political tumult in Berlin and other German cities in the early days of the republican government. The Free Corps of former officers restored order with little difficulty, and elections for the Constituent Assembly were held in the normal way. There were short-lived Bolshevik governments in Hungary and Bavaria, both supported only by small minorities, both overthrown in a short time. There was considerable disorder in Italy, largely fomented by the forces that claimed to be putting it down.

This wholesale defeat of Bolshevism was often attributed solely to military force or black reaction. Actually, the situation was a good deal more complicated. The war was supposed to have shaken the foundations of civilized life, and so it did, in countries where the war was run badly. In countries which managed the war better, war actually strengthened the social order. The most efficient wartime governments, such as the British government of Lloyd George and even, to some extent, the German government, conciliated the masses. They promoted welfare, and this continued to operate after the war. In these more advanced countries, the war lessened the class conflict instead of increasing it. A general strike in Great Britain before the war would have been accompanied by violence. In 1926 it was a harmless operation. Thus, the war had contradictory effects: Bolshevism in Russia, a more secure society elsewhere.

Outside politics, certainly, there was no marked increase in violence: rather the reverse. Murders and criminal assaults were no more frequent than before, while on the other hand some states abolished capital punishment. Human behaviour was gentler. Women could walk the streets unattended, something they had hesitated to do before the war. The police no longer shunned certain districts after nightfall. People were kinder to children and more concerned about their welfare. People were kinder to animals. Brutal sports declined even in England, their most obstinate home.

The most powerful civilized habit was the habit of buying and selling, particularly the habit of buying and selling labour. In the days of gold currency, men knew what they were getting when they sold; after the war, they could not be so sure. In a few countries, the paper currencies tumbled to nothing for a brief period, and there was an occasional return to barter. Even then, workers still went to

Reichsbanknote

Zwei Millionen Mark

A — T

zahlt die Reichsbankhauptkasse in Berlin gegen diese Banknote dem Einlieferer. Vom 1. September 1923 ab kann diese Banknote aufgerufen und unter Umtausch gegen andere gesetzliche Zahlungsmittel eingezogen werden

Berlin, den 9. August 1923

Reichsbankdirektorium

Wer Banknoten nachmacht oder verfälscht oder nachgemachte oder verfälschte sich verschafft und in Verkehr bringt, wird mit Zuchthaus nicht unter zwei Jahren bestraft

033231

48, 49 Symbols of inflation. German mark notes of 1922 and 1923

the factories, and clerks to their office desks. Very few Europeans imagined that they could keep alive only by grabbing what they needed. Trains still ran across Europe in an orderly fashion. Telephones still functioned. Letters from abroad reached their destinations in Russia even at the height of the revolution. Nowhere outside Russia was there famine, though there was often grave shortage after the destruction and upset of war. Europe, in fact, remained a civilized community despite alarms to the contrary. Civilization was held together by the civilized behaviour of ordinary people. Writers saw only woe in the so-called rise of the masses, but in reality the masses were calmer and more sensible than those who ruled over them. While formal religion went down, conscience went up. There was never a time when men worried more over the question of whether they were doing right, though they were perhaps never more at a loss to know by what standards right and wrong should be judged.

Men often lamented the supposedly happy conditions which had existed before August 1914. On the other hand, many of them, particularly in the victorious countries, imagined that a better world would spring almost automatically from the war. The peace conference, which met at Paris early in 1919, was widely expected to establish the reign of Peace and Justice. President Wilson was regarded, not only by himself, as a latter-day Saviour from the New World. Disillusionment followed. Wilson was alleged to have been bamboozled by Lloyd George and Clemenceau. Yet Wilson's own practice was strikingly undemocratic for a democratic statesman. He had championed self-determination. The Allies had claimed to be fighting for the independence of small nations, and every nation, down to the smallest, duly sent its delegation to the peace conference. These delegations were rarely consulted and never allowed to decide. The Big Three set themselves up as the dictators of Europe, indeed of the world, more ruthlessly than Napoleon I and Tsar Alexander I had done at the height of their power. But orders from the top were increasingly disregarded, and Europe settled down as much despite the three great men as thanks to their labours.

The prize exhibit of the settlement was the League of Nations, an innovation, it was hoped, of immeasurable significance. For the first time, modern man recognized an authority which transcended the sovereign state. The authority of the League was purely moral. The member states remained sovereign, and the League could operate only with their consent. Nevertheless, the League was expected gradually to overshadow its members. Recourse to the League would become a habit; national conflicts would be tamed; war would fall out of fashion, as duelling had done. Yet the very powers who created the League failed to demonstrate their faith in it. They continued to maintain their own armed forces and relied on these when their interests were threatened. Wilson, who had been the most determined in creating the League, was also the most insistent in limiting its powers for the sake of American opinion. The limitations were not enough, and the United States did not join the League of Nations. This has often been lamented, but the record of American policy suggests that, if the United States had been in the League, they might have made that body even more ineffective.

The United States, despite their abstention, had great influence on the League, which came after a great European war and was constructed mainly to meet European conditions. It would perhaps have made sense as an organ for European conciliation. But it was assumed at the peace conference that the United States must come in and, if so, the rest of the world could not be left out. All countries great and small, except for the former enemies, were bustled into the League without delay. Geneva was presented as an embryonic world capital, where European procedures and habits of mind would set a pattern for all the world – a curious, belated flicker of the assumption that Europe alone possessed the secret of civilization.

The League of Nations was to prove unsuccessful as an instrument for preventing war. Indeed, it did not manage to settle even trivial disputes between its members, unless the disputants had rigged the solution privately beforehand. It was a portent all the same, a fumbling attempt to create some loyalty higher than that of the sovereign state, and it represented a new morality which men thought should apply to others, even if they did not apply it to themselves.

Characteristically, the League spirit was contradicted by the other prize exhibit of the peace conference: the achievement of self-determination or, put more crudely, of national states. As a matter of fact, this was not the work of the peace conference. The national states achieved their own existence before the peace conference met, and the statesmen could only regulate some details of their frontiers. The new states wrought a considerable transformation of European affairs. Though nationalism had been a feature of European civilization for a long time, France was in 1914 the only important European state where it was the sole basis of loyalty. In the others, loyalty to the monarch – King, Emperor, Tsar, or Kaiser – came first, and national sentiment was a relatively late addition. Indeed, national sentiment was often a disruptive force, as in Ireland, most of Austria-Hungary, and the lands inhabited by Poles. At the end of the war many monarchs lost their thrones, and nearly every state was constituted on a national basis. Loyalty no longer went to an individual, except perhaps to the King of England. It went to an impersonal Nation.

National feeling was not only stronger than before: there were also more nations. Before 1914 a highly cultured man could get by if he knew the output in six European languages of historic fame – English, French, German, Italian, Russian, Spanish. By 1919 he needed to know also Czech, Hungarian, Polish, and Rumanian – probably Croat and Slovak as well. Prague, Budapest, and Warsaw were all cities of European stature. Modern music, for instance, would have lost half its resources without them. The less advanced nations aspired to the same achievement. Every nation boasted its national culture, wanted its national army and its national tariffs. There were national theatres and national opera houses, often very distinguished, in every capital. Art of every kind was more national in character than it had been before.

The establishment of the new national states seemed to involve a disintegration of European unity. There was a widespread idea, particularly in the large historic countries, that small states were necessarily weak and poor. A glance at Switzerland might have suggested some doubt, and for that matter China, the most populous country in the world, was by no means the richest or the most powerful. The tariff walls which the new states set up certainly

50 The peacemakers. Sir William Orpen's painting of the signing of the Peace of Versailles on 28 June 1919

51, 52, 53 Nationalism in Art. The National Theatre in Prague (above); figures carved by the German, Ernst Barlach, for St Catherine's in Lübeck (bottom left); the manuscript score of an opera by the Czech composer Leoš Janáček (bottom right)

54 The auditorium
of the Berlin
Grosses Schauspielhaus,
designed by
Hans Poelzig
for the great director,
Max Reinhardt,
and built in 1919

disrupted the existing economic order of Europe, but they also enabled the new states to develop their own industries. The rate of economic growth in independent Czechoslovakia, for instance, was a good deal higher than it had been under the Habsburgs. In the old pattern, western Europe, broadly speaking, was industrialized; eastern Europe was not. By changing this pattern, the new national states ensured that Europe, though more divided into nations, was also taking on a more common form. The ostensible grievance against them was that they were backward. Their real fault, maybe, was that they did not strive even harder against their backwardness.

There was no doubt a grave casualty, though this could hardly be blamed on the new states. This casualty was the European Balance of Power. At one time, to outward appearance even in 1914, there had been four or five Great Powers in Europe. Now Austria-

67

Hungary had gone for good, and Russia had vanished temporarily. The new states developed their own armies, largely with French assistance. They formed alliances, again largely at French prompting. But they could not take the place of the former Great Powers. After all, Germany had seemed to be on the way to overshadowing Europe even when these Powers existed. The war, whatever its origins, had turned into a struggle against German supremacy and was therefore evidence that the Balance of Power had broken down. The outcome of the war emphasized still more Germany's position in Europe.

This position was politically the greatest problem in Europe between the wars. And not only politically. The facts of geography and economics demanded that Germany should be brought fully into the European community. Otherwise Europe would hardly exist except as a name on the maps. The way to reconciliation seemed to be open. The Allies had claimed to be defending democracy against German imperialism. Now the Germans had accepted the ideals of the victors. The Kaiser had gone, and the German republic had, on paper, the most perfect of democratic constitutions. It had a Socialist president, Ebert, and the Social Democrats were the largest single party in the Reichstag.

Nevertheless, the reconciliation did not take place. Many of the victorious statesmen, particularly in France, wanted to shift on to Germany the costs of the war and therefore could not admit that she had purged her guilt. The peoples could not forget, in a few months, the passions and hatreds of wartime. They alleged that the democratic transformation was mere sleight-of-hand, to escape merited punishment. Most Germans, even most Social Democrats, remained stalwart patriots. On the other hand, the Allied statesmen regarded with even more suspicion the few Left-wing Germans who preached pacifism and internationalism – ideas associated, however falsely, with Bolshevism.

The peace settlement with Germany was therefore a combination of opposites, like so much that was done at Paris. The Germans were treated harshly. The settlement was imposed on them virtually without negotiation, certainly without verbal negotiation – a unique case in modern times. Germany's armaments were rigorously restricted;

she had to accept an undefined obligation to pay reparations; her western territory, the Rhineland, was occupied by Allied forces. At the same time, the settlement assumed that Germany would ultimately be reconciled. The Germans were assured that they could join the League of Nations once they had demonstrated their reformed character, and even the most severe terms of the treaty, such as reparations, could work only with German co-operation. The Allied statesmen seem to have supposed that the Germans would recognize the moral validity of the treaty once they had set their names to it – a conception which worked in the world of business affairs, but less often in politics. There was no attempt to dismember Germany, as there might have been in previous centuries. Germany lost only territory which was inhabited by peoples of other nationalities – a little to Denmark, a good deal to Poland. The guiding principle was justice, not security, though this did not make the losses any more palatable to the Germans. German Austria was forbidden to unite with Germany – an infringement, perhaps, of self-determination. Otherwise Germany emerged intact, still indisputably a power of the first rank once she had recovered from her temporary weakness.

The peacemakers realized that they had not done well in their settlement with Germany. Each of them recorded his dissatisfaction one way or another. The Americans soon withdrew from the political affairs of Europe. Lloyd George, as the voice of the British, hoped vaguely that the treaty would be revised. The French hoped, still more vaguely, that it would be enforced. Still, there was a settlement of a sort, and the German problem became a matter of negotiation for the next twenty years. The great men at Paris were less successful with Russia. The Supreme Council made some feeble efforts to intervene against the Bolsheviks. They also made some feeble efforts to get on better terms. Both efforts failed. By 1920 the Soviet government controlled all the former territories of Imperial Russia except for the Baltic states and the western lands which were lost to Poland. Thus Russia, though racked by famine and economic chaos, remained implicitly a Great Power. The so-called capitalist world, in impotent resentment, simply refused to acknowledge what had happened. Soviet Russia was denied diplomatic recognition, as though this would wish her out of existence, and Europe was left permanently out of balance, its entire eastern wing cut off.

The Bolsheviks contributed to their own isolation. They repudiated the obligations of previous Russian governments in both politics and finance. They believed that their Socialist system was in perpetual war with the capitalist countries, a war which must be fought to final victory one way or the other. Hence they regarded it as a waste of time to strive for agreement except on the most temporary basis. The Bolsheviks were not cast down by the failure of their original hope that the walls of capitalist Jericho would collapse overnight. At Lenin's guidance they waited with a little extra patience for the supposedly inevitable crisis. When the war ended, it seemed that they had not waited in vain. Much of Europe was in turmoil and confusion. Surely it would be easy to repeat elsewhere the Bolshevik success. In the summer of 1919 the Bolsheviks set up the Third, or Communist, International. The representatives of other countries were a scratch lot, hastily brought together. But this did not matter: the urgent thing was to provide some central direction for the revolutions which were about to break out. Once again the Bolshevik hopes were disappointed. Soviet governments in Hungary and Bavaria were crushed. The others did not come into existence.

55 Russian peasants wait for bread during the famine of 1921

56 The new apostles. Lenin in the presidium of the First Comintern Congress in the Kremlin

A year later, however, the Bolsheviks thought they had another chance. The counter-revolutionary forces having been defeated, the Red Army was sweeping into Poland. The Bolsheviks imagined that they would be welcomed as liberators, as the French Jacobins had been. The second Congress of the Communist International was a more substantial affair than the first, with genuine delegates representing more or less genuine parties. It seemed a rival version, on a different basis, of the Supreme Council which had recently met in Paris: the general staff of a coming world revolution. Hopes were dashed for the third time. The Red Army faltered in front of Warsaw and was driven back. A humiliating peace was concluded with Poland. Early in 1921 Lenin decided to retreat at home as he had done in international affairs. The New Economic Policy relaxed the rigours of war Communism. The Communist Party, as it was now called, retained a monopoly of political power in a country where the economic bases for Socialism hardly existed – a flagrant contradiction of Marxist principles. The Communists, including Lenin, were again waiting, though they did not know for what. For a new bout of revolutions? Or for the creation of Socialism in Russia?

71

Their theory told them that it must be the first; practice gradually led them towards the second. After all, they could, with enormous effort, do something to change Russia's economic life. They could do little to provoke revolutions elsewhere.

This record of disappointed hopes reinforced Russia's isolation. The capitalist countries were angered by the Communist talk of provoking revolution; and the Communists, exaggerating their own threats, believed that they were equally threatened by a war of counter-revolution. Threats bred suspicion, and suspicion bred more threats. No one on either side then could imagine that Russia might merely settle down again into being a European Great Power, behaving as other Great Powers did. Instead, there was supposed to be an impassable cleavage between Soviet Russia and the rest of the world, a cleavage of ideas as well as of policy. In conventional opinion, Russia had relapsed into primitive barbarism, and the Bolsheviks were 'baboons', as Churchill called them. Admirers, such as the Fabian writers, Sidney and Beatrice Webb, discovered in Soviet Russia 'a new civilization'.

In fact, the practice of Russian government was not much different from what it had been in the days of the Tsar. The theory of Communism, on the other hand, was almost entirely west European, not Russian, in origin. Its philosophy stemmed from Marx and Engels. The Bolshevik revolution itself, in its early days, differed from attempts elsewhere only in being successful – a result of chance and geography, not of superior method. Nearly all the Communist leaders except Stalin had spent most of their adult life outside Russia and had been deeply involved in the general affairs of European Socialism. They did not abandon these interests when they attained power in Russia; on the contrary, they valued that power largely because it would give them a greater voice in affairs abroad. One might suppose, for instance, that Lenin would have been fully occupied in 1919 with the civil war and economic chaos inside Russia. Not at all. He followed the affairs of foreign Socialist parties throughout Europe and peered over into Asia. His only literary production of the year was a pedantic little book, in which he argued that British Communists ought to join the Labour Party.

57 The gradualists at home. Sidney and Beatrice Webb, intellectual admirers of the Soviet Union

Again, all the Bolshevik leaders, except perhaps Stalin, took an extremely active part in the Communist International and by no means treated it as an instrument of Soviet policy. Rather, they regarded Russia as an instrument for helping international revolution. Moscow, far from being their spiritual home or final objective, was intended as a mere wayside junction on the road to more important European capitals. Outside politics, Soviet Russia was a show-piece of advanced European ideas. No country experimented more adventurously in education and in the treatment of criminals. Divorce by consent was introduced – an enlightened step transformed by anti-Bolshevik propaganda into the nationalization of women. Throughout the 1920s Meyerhold was the most exciting theatrical director in Europe, and about the same time the film directors Eisenstein and Pudovkin stepped into the first place as leaders of creative cinema.

73

58, 59, 60 The flowering of new Russian art. Left, a still from the film *Aelita*, with sets by Ravinovitch and costumes by Alexandra Exter, 1919–20. Above, the most famous scene

Of course, Soviet Russia remained a dictatorship, with political power tightly held by the leaders of the Communist Party. Still, there was very little arbitrary rule in the period after the civil wars, and western Europeans who visited Russia – say, about the time of Lenin's death in 1924 – could be excused for seeing there a sketch for the Socialist countries of the future. At the other extreme, the representatives of the old order disliked Soviet Russia as much for the good things as for the bad, or perhaps even more. If the Soviet revolution had been merely a fraud and had produced merely dictatorship and terror, the established authorities of Europe would soon have accepted it. They were estranged by the fear that there was in Soviet Russia a genuine element of social change and even of Socialist creation. They denounced Communism as an alien idea or even as a conspiracy. They were really alarmed that support for Communism

from Eisenstein's famous film *Battleship Potemkin*. Below, a 1922 stage production by Meyerhold

existed in most of the European states. The Communist parties of western Europe were not, in fact, invented by Soviet Russia, though they were later subsidized by it. On the contrary, they grew naturally out of what had been the Left Wing of longstanding Socialist parties.

The establishment of the Third International certainly had an effect, not in stimulating Communist movements elsewhere, but in provoking an open breach between revolutionary and moderate Socialists, who had previously been members of the same party. The two groups had wrangled continuously ever since Marx's day, but they had wrangled within a common framework. Each had affected the other. The revolutionaries had been made less revolutionary; the moderates had been made less moderate. The open split into two Internationals drove them apart. The Communists were pushed further and further into intransigence. No Communist, for instance, became a member of any European government, except in Spain, until after the Second World War. The moderates became more concerned to fight Communists than to fight capitalism and moved everywhere towards co-operation, conscious or otherwise, with the *bourgeois* parties. The traditional name for all Socialists, a name endorsed by Marx himself, was Social Democrats. Before the First World War the emphasis was on their Socialism, after it, on their democracy; and democracy itself was often a euphemism for anti-Communism.

Democracy had, of course, a more serious meaning. It stood for the combination of political freedom and universal suffrage, with an emphasis on the former; freedom of expression – that is, freedom for organized meetings and newspapers not controlled by the government; freedom of movement and of trade-union action; and the rule of law – that is, the acceptance of existing judicial bodies as impartial institutions detached from the class struggle. Democracy meant, perhaps above all, the willing acceptance of majority decisions according to the existing constitutions, even when these decisions went against Socialism. The Social Democrats were buoyed up by the belief that, since they represented the working classes (or so they claimed), the decision of the majority would one day go their way – 'the inevitability of gradualness', as Webb called it. They were content to wait

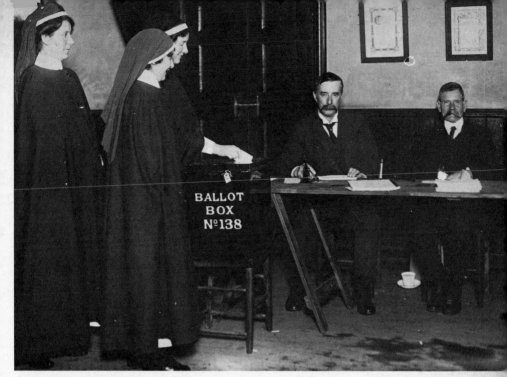

61 Women rewarded. Nurses casting their vote in the General Election of December 1918

until that happened, and they laid more emphasis on waiting than in ensuring that it should happen.

This is not to say that the democracy of post-war Europe had no real content. In many ways Europe became democratic as it had never been before. This was obviously true in a formal sense. There were now twelve republics in Europe where previously there had been only two. Nearly every country had universal suffrage, with Hungary as the flagrant exception, and even where dictatorships were later set up, as they often were, these arbitrary governments (including even that of Soviet Russia) usually claimed to speak and act for the masses, not for some king or emperor. Even the few monarchs who retained or recovered personal power, such as the King of Yugoslavia, were popular dictators rather than rulers of the old sort. Some monarchs, particularly the King of England, perhaps acquired increased importance as national symbols, but their political power seems usually to have decreased.

62 'You Can Trust Me', the slogan of Stanley Baldwin during the 1922 General Election

The eclipse of aristocracy was even more total. The First World War virtually completed the decline of the privileged governing class – a decline which had been going on ever since the French Revolution. That class had owed its position to two factors – hereditary rank and landed possessions – both of which were now challenged. In some countries hereditary titles were abolished. In others, such as France, they lingered only as empty social adornments. The British aristocracy still exercised some political power in the House of Lords, but that power had been formally reduced by the Parliament Act of 1911 and, what was more important, the old families there were increasingly swamped by newly created peers, few of whom were of aristocratic birth. Very few aristocrats occupied important ministerial posts in the inter-war period. Every German Chancellor before 1914, for instance, had been ostensibly of noble birth; in the inter-war period none was, with the trivial exceptions of von Papen and von Schleicher. The three British Conservative leaders – Bonar Law, Baldwin, Neville Chamberlain – were all unmistakably capitalists, not aristocrats, and those British aristocrats who remained in politics usually had to display *bourgeois* habits of industry and application.

The economic decline of aristocracy was also considerable, though not complete. Most of the new states in east-central Europe carried through land reforms, by which the great estates were broken up among peasant proprietors. The Austrian aristocracy ceased to exist, as did, of course, the Russian aristocracy under the impact of the Bolshevik revolution. Great landed proprietors survived in Hungary and Poland, but few of them could count on secure wealth. The Prussian Junkers east of the Elbe were a special case. Economically, their enterprise was no longer profitable, but even the German republic regarded them, for some reason, as socially desirable, and the Junker estates were repeatedly kept from ruin by concealed subsidies. Probably the British aristocracy made out best. Some of their great families remained wealthy, thanks to two quirks of English law – coal royalties and urban ground-rents. Even so, their fortunes were less than those made in industry. The richest man in England at the beginning of the twentieth century was the Duke of Devonshire. After the war he was outclassed by a shipowner, Sir John Ellerman.

63 British fashion in 1928, during the flapper era. Flower garden frocks modelled at Ascot

The aristocracy counted only as a trivial entertainment, providing material for gossip-columns and photographs in glossy magazines. Surveying Europe immediately after the First World War, an observer might well suppose that the ideas of the French Revolution had finally triumphed.

This victory of democracy proved a false dawn. Many of the countries which became apparently democratic in 1919 did not remain so for long. Organized freedom needed habits of tolerance and order which were rare outside western Europe. It needed an educated middle-class *élite*, which was also in short supply. Peasant leaders could win political power, but they were unlikely to observe the rules of integrity or fair play. Czechoslovakia was the only new state *bourgeois* enough to remain a democracy on the French model. In Germany there was an *élite* which had been powerful in the days of the empire, and it never genuinely accepted the new order. As a result, the Weimar republic had a precarious existence, fully supported only by the Social Democrats and a few middle-class converts. Stresemann was the chief of these, perhaps the most typical figure of the 1920s. Though an ardent patriot, indeed an imperialist, Stresemann aspired to make Germany great again within the framework of democracy, just as he practised fulfilment and peaceful revision in international affairs. Stresemann was that rare thing – a good German. Among active German politicians, outside the Social Democrats, he was more than rare: he was unique.

The greatest set-back for democracy was in Italy. Here was a western European country, with a reasonable tradition of constitutional life and an acknowledged position as a Great Power. Its post-war troubles were little worse than those of France or Great Britain, but they provoked a more violent response. A renegade Socialist, Mussolini, used the opportunity to create the Fascist Party – a movement of action which brought the methods of war into civil politics. The Fascists provoked disorder so that they could then claim to put it down, and in 1922 Mussolini exploited the confusion among the political parties to establish himself as authoritarian ruler of Italy. Mussolini did not seize power by revolution, despite the myth of a march on Rome. He intrigued himself into power and launched the

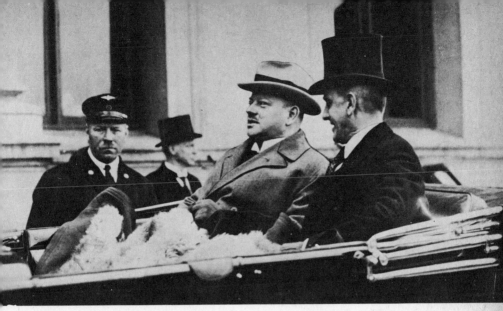

64 The good German. Dr Stresemann in Oslo, where he received the Nobel Peace Prize
in 1926

myth afterwards. Until 1925 he was precariously placed, and the
discredit following on the murder of a Socialist deputy, Matteotti, by
Fascist thugs, threatened to bring him down. Mussolini survived the
crisis, and from this time the Fascist Party became the only political
organization in the country. Fascism was revolution from above: a
planned destruction of freedom by men who already controlled all
the power in the state. Fascism was also revolution by fraud: talk
without action. There was no new policy, no social transformation,
only dictatorship for its own sake. Mussolini lived for show. He did
little. Through destruction of the trade unions, capitalists had an easy
time of it. Some intellectuals disliked the encroachment on their
freedom of thought. Otherwise Fascism provided only display:
marches, rhetoric, fancy dress.

This was not how it appeared at the time. Many men were
obsessed by fear of Communism and saw in Fascism the salvation of
society. Writers who had shown their cleverness by railing at democracy discovered in Fascism the answer to their wit. Ezra Pound
became a Fascist. Bernard Shaw, though an inveterate Fabian Socialist, followed him close. On the other side, radicals used Fascism as a

81

65 The new Italian. Mussolini in a typical pose in 1928

66 Fascists transported. Cyclists salute Mussolini during 1923 celebrations

term of abuse for those more conservative than themselves. Authoritarian régimes of the old sort were equated with Mussolini's demagogic dictatorship, and the Fascist label was stuck on them. Marxists announced that Fascism was the last stage of capitalism in decline and foretold that every capitalist class would adopt it, but little came of this. Germany, a decade later, was to take up with Fascism of a rather different form; other than that, there was no effective Fascist movement outside Italy. Fascism contributed little to European civilization except the melancholy reflection that the Italy of Garibaldi and Mazzini had become the Italy of Mussolini.

The melancholy was not great in the days when Mussolini still wore a top hat and attended international conferences. Five years or so after the end of the war, Europe seemed to have reached a new stability. The paper currencies which had oscillated so widely once more took on a resemblance to gold. The inflation which hit most European countries left its mark. The secure savings of the cautious middle class lost much or all of their value, whereas the holdings of the great capitalists were undiminished. This weakening of the middle class is said to have contributed to the political instability of the following decade, and probably it did – but the process was not all one way. While the middle class was becoming less firmly

anchored, the classes above and below it were more and more taking on its ways. More and more people in Europe looked and thought *bourgeois*. Indeed, Europeans were the *bourgeoisie* of the world. Mussolini paraded Italy's grievance as 'a proletarian nation'. The true proletarian nations were to be found in the starving peoples of the East. European civilization had brought for them an escape from death. It did not bring them an escape into a better life.

Europe's continuing hold on the outer world was one of the most surprising features in the inter-war period. The World War was supposed to have reflected discredit on European civilization, and the European powers seemed to have lost much of their material strength. They were alarmed that their empires were crumbling, though the alarm was exaggerated. Great Britain and France did not merely hang on to their existing possessions, they added new ones, particularly from the spoils of Turkey. Great Britain dominated the Middle East from Cyprus and Egypt to the Persian Gulf and found a new source of wealth in the exploitation of its oil-wells. The economic

67, 68 Labourers, German and British. Left, a woodcut by Franz Masreel; right, a strike of coalminers at Wigan in 1921

preponderance of Europe was also renewed in a modified form. Some countries outside Europe – particularly the United States and Japan – had greatly increased their industrial strength during the war and were now formidable competitors of the old exporting powers. But most countries had increased still more their output of primary products – food and raw materials – in order to meet the insatiable demands of the belligerents. After the war the price of these primary products fell catastrophically, while the price of industrial goods remained high. The terms of trade changed dramatically in Europe's favour. Fewer exports bought more imports. The advantage was not all one way. The industrial countries satisfied their needs with less work, but on the other hand, their overseas consumers were impoverished, and it became harder to find markets.

The result was prosperity and unemployment side by side – the characteristic feature of the inter-war period. Those who had work were better off than before, and those who employed them still more so. Against this, there were always more out of work, even in the most flourishing times. The unemployed in Great Britain never fell below 10 per cent of the employed population between 1921 and 1939. In Germany the proportion of unemployed was even greater – never less than 13·6 per cent. This unemployment was not caused only by the failure of overseas markets; the home market, too, did not expand, or not enough to absorb the increased capacity of industrial production. The unemployed received meagre assistance or none at all. Wages remained stable while productive power was going up. The greatest symbol of this was the unsuccessful general strike in Great Britain in 1926. Though this was launched in order to prevent reductions of wages in the coal industry, its failure meant that there would be no increase of wages anywhere. In earlier times, the surplus population of Europe escaped by going overseas. Now most of the world, particularly the United States, closed the door against European immigrants. The peoples of Europe were bottled up in their own continent. The stage was being set for a great economic explosion: more goods than before and no more buyers.

The explosion needed some years to stoke up, and in the meantime Europe enjoyed the illusion of a return to normal. There were no more attempts at revolution after 1923. The Communist International resigned itself to a long period of waiting. Germany formally accepted the new order in Europe, or so it seemed. In 1924 she agreed to pay reparations according to the Dawes plan, and the following year she signed the Treaty of Locarno with her former enemies. The frontier between France and Germany was demilitarized and guaranteed by Great Britain and Italy. In 1926 Germany was admitted to the League of Nations and given a permanent seat on the Council, along with the other Great Powers. The Disarmament Commission was withdrawn from Germany, as a demonstration of belief, not altogether well founded, in her good faith. Currencies were once more freely interchangeable. The international trains again ran across Europe with only brief stops at the frontiers. Though passports were now universally required – a lamentable legacy of the war – most European countries abandoned visas by the middle of the decade. It was once more possible for men to imagine that national antagonisms were fading away.

69 Bank clerks defy the London General Strike of 1926

The war, in fact, had given men a fright, without destroying their settled habits. The social patterns of private life changed little. All Europeans, except for a few Turks, held to monogamous marriage: one man married one woman, usually on the basis of mutual affection, and it was assumed that they would remain together for life. Virtually all children in virtually all European countries received some education. Women somewhat improved their position; indeed, some observers have claimed that the emancipation of women was the greatest social result of the First World War. Perhaps this is an exaggeration. Women got the vote in many European countries, though by no means in all. Many professions were opened to them, and more women than before worked in industry or in offices. On the other hand, the man remained the head of the family – always in law, normally in practice. It was still most unusual for a husband to share the housework, except perhaps in the British middle class. But the gravest burden of women was lessened. The birth-rate declined in every European country, and most in those with the highest standard of life. By the 1930s, every country except

70, 71, 72 Carriers of civilization in 1925. The Austin Chummy Tourer, the Morris Oxford
two-seater and the Morris two-seater

the Netherlands and Portugal looked forward (wrongly, as it turned
out) to a time when the population would not be reproducing itself.
We do not know at all precisely the reasons for this decline, and still
less the means by which it was achieved, but the fact of fewer births
is undeniable. It clearly involved a revolution at the very basis of
human life.

There were other changes in spheres remote from politics. The
greatest was the coming of the automobile or motor-car. This was
not only a transformation: it was an emancipation. For thousands of
years, ever since the invention of the wheel, men in a hurry could
move only at the speed of horses. In the nineteenth century railways
had put the speed up from 8 or 10 miles an hour to 50, but men were
still shackled to the iron frame of the rails and the communal travel
of the carriages. In towns, electric trams provided a similar, more
local pattern, and tramways reached their greatest extent as late as
1928. Their heyday was short, for the internal combustion engine
was enabling men to go at a high speed whenever they wanted to
and in any direction where roads existed. People were freed from
timetables, and from having to co-operate with others, except in
the negative sense of not running them down. Every possessor of a
motor-car enjoyed a freedom previously known only by the gods.

The early automobiles were large, elegant, and expensive; they
are now prized possessions in museums. Henry Ford was the first to
produce an automobile for general use. But his Tin Lizzie, though
certainly cheap, was designed for the great expanses of the American

73 An electric tram in Berlin. This was the most common form of public transport in all European cities

continent. Two British firms, Morris and Austin, took the lead in producing vehicles which were small as well as cheap. By the end of the 1920s, there were already over a million motor-cars in Great Britain. Continental Europe moved more slowly. Still, the motor-car became an accepted sight even here and no longer produced a sensation, except perhaps in remote Balkan villages. The surfaces of main roads throughout western and central Europe were made fit for motor traffic by the end of the 1920s. Italy was first in the field with special motorways, and Germany followed in Hitler's time.

The social impact of the automobile was still on a limited scale. It was used mainly for pleasure and, to some extent, for holidays. Michelin, the French tyre firm, produced annually a guide to hotels for tourists. The guide was distinguished by its assessment of hotel meals, and this made it a sacred document of contemporary civilization in later years. But commercial travellers, for instance, still worked their districts from the nearest railway station. The automobile had not yet become a vehicle for daily transport, taking the businessman to his office, still less the worker to his factory. Far from being a common possession, it was a dividing line between classes, as also between the more advanced industrial nations and the more backward east European communities.

The workings of the automobile revolution showed themselves sooner in public transport – buses on regular services, charabancs for occasional tours. Urban transport was still provided mainly by electric trams, with buses only as an extra, faster service. But buses could go everywhere; they were not confined to tram lines and could run from the towns into country districts. The distinction between town and country, which had existed since the beginning of civilization, began to disappear. Those who worked in towns could live in the country, and country-dwellers could more easily use the services of the neighbouring towns. Fewer people lived in the centres of towns – a tendency very strong in Great Britain, where the industrial towns, in particular, lost much of their heart. The tendency was general, though not so strong, in France and western Germany, while it had hardly begun farther east.

Motor vehicles were used also for the delivery of supplies, especially of foodstuffs. Covent Garden and Les Halles now depended on motor lorries, not on horse vans. In England the milk trains declined and soon ceased. Human beings were also delivered increasingly by motor transport: the taxi took the place of the fiacre and the hansom cab in most capital cities. Altogether, there was a revolutionary transformation in human life. The horse, which had been an essential element in civilization since the earliest times, now became a luxury or an adornment of public displays. Rich people still rode horses for pleasure, and horse-racing went on in every country, but there were

74 Slow motion. The advent of motor transport produced traffic scenes such as this in the Strand, London, as early as 1923

few horses in the streets of cities. The pedestrian no longer had to cope with mud and dirt – his problem was how to escape the motor traffic when he crossed the streets. The triumph of the automobile had one strange exception. Armies had learned to rely on railways. The more advanced of them were equipped with armoured motor vehicles, the tanks. They neglected mechanized transport for the infantry. Even on the eve of the Second World War, generals still wore riding-boots, not mechanics' overalls.

The internal combustion engine had rather different results in the air. Here, too, it brought a revolution: men attained their age-old dream and were able to fly. It caused a sensation before the First World War when men flew across the English Channel or even got off the ground at all. After the war, longer flights provided further sensations. Two British aviators, Alcock and Brown, crossed the Atlantic; others flew to India and then on to Australia. An American, Charles Lindbergh, flew across the Atlantic alone and achieved lasting fame as the representative of the new age. Yet very little of a practical kind followed. The aeroplane did not become a normal method of travel in the inter-war years: the existing machines were too unreliable, the costs still too high. On the other hand, the aeroplane was fully accepted as a weapon of war, in theory if not in practice. Some authorities claimed that future wars could be won by air-power alone. Some even foretold that aerial bombing would bring universal destruction. Most men still held to the old belief that advance in any direction must necessarily be an improvement.

Electricity came second in importance only to the motor-car in the social effects it produced. Here again, the result was emancipation from manual labour and physical drudgery. Homes could be lit at

75 New source of power. A hydro-electric station built in 1921 at Mühleberg, Switzerland

76 First across. ...ock and Brown in front of the plane in which they spanned the Atlantic

the turn of a switch instead of by candles and oil-lamps. In the cities, every street could be illuminated by a single master-switch, whereas previously the lamp-lighter had had to trudge from one lamp-post to the next. Electrical power enabled factories to be built in or near the big cities which consumed their goods, instead of near the coalfields; and countries which had previously suffered from lack of coal, such as Switzerland and Italy, now developed factories driven from hydro-electric stations. Civilized life was made easier and brighter. It was also more democratic. Electricity was an economic proposition only if everyone, or nearly everyone, used it. Soon the humblest homes were more brightly lit than the grandest palaces of previous ages. The process took, of course, a long time to complete. The countryside lagged behind the towns in supply of electricity. Coal fires were still the rule for most homes in the inter-war years. Electrical devices other than lighting were rare: vacuum cleaners were coming in, but washing-machines and refrigerators were hardly known.

77 Proud broadcasters. Shayle Gardener and Hubert Carter face a transmitter at Marconi House in 1923

One offshoot of electricity had a special impact on social life. This was the transmission of messages by wireless waves, 'broadcasting' or 'radio', as it came to be called. Wireless telegraphy had been invented early in the century and was widely used during the First World War, particularly at sea. The sounds sent out were the dot-and-dash of Morse code, and the service was no more than an extension of the ordinary telegraph. After the war, sounds were directly transmitted to private receiving-sets, activated by electricity, which then reproduced them through loudspeakers. In nearly all European countries, this broadcasting was controlled, directly or indirectly, by the state, and so might have been expected to become a powerful weapon of political propaganda. It did so to some extent in the non-democratic countries, such as Italy, Russia, and later Germany. Some democratic statesmen owed their reputation largely to their mastery of the microphone, as witness Stanley Baldwin in

Great Britain. More often, the broadcasting of news and political affairs managed to remain neutral or, it would be truer to say, innocuous.

The prime function of the radio was entertainment: the broadcasting of plays or music, particularly light music, which flowed in an almost endless stream. This was entertainment in the home, and passive entertainment at that. The listener had only to turn a few knobs. Most Europeans spent more of their time in their more comfortable homes. The traditional forms of entertainment – public houses, clubs, music halls – tended to decline, or at best remained stable. Broadcasting made the European less of a social animal than he had been before. On the other hand, there were fewer institutions and activities interposed between the individual and the nation. A man was now either sitting alone with his family or else listening to the same programme as every other Englishman, Frenchman, or German. Holland was the only country which had four different types of programme, provided by four different sectarian bodies (Roman Catholic, Strict Protestant, Liberal Protestant, and agnostic).

78 The listening public. A radio (left of the fireplace) became a fixture of almost all households during the 'twenties

79, 80 The world's lover and the world's sweetheart, Rudolph Valentino and Mary Pickford

There was, however, another new force which pulled people out of their homes even more powerfully than broadcasting kept them in. The cinema, too, was a recent invention which reached maturity after the First World War – though the films were silent, that is, not synchronized with sound, until the end of the decade. Americans had come to dominate the market during the war years, and Hollywood became the unchallenged centre of film-production. American film-stars enjoyed wider fame than any human beings before. Mary Pickford was the world's sweetheart. All the world mourned the death of Rudolph Valentino, the great lover. The American cinema was dominated by a few great monopolies and was designed for mass-audiences. Though its ideas and emotions were crude, simple, and banal, it often became a serious form of art. Charlie Chaplin was not only a clown and a commercial success: he was also a great artist. The little man whom he created survives as the best symbol of the age. Academic writers announced the arrival of the masses; Chaplin's little man asserted the unique character of every individual.

The films shown in the cinema provided art for the masses, by no means always on the principle of the lowest common denominator. The buildings themselves in which films were shown displayed mass architecture of the worst kind; none is ever likely to attract support from even the most zealous preservationist. Still, these glittering palaces provided imperial grandeur for everybody. This was entertainment on a new scale. The cinemas were cheaper than previous places of entertainment, they were more comfortable, they were open for longer hours. And they were everywhere – in every town and in many villages. They were also for everybody, without distinction of class, age, or sex. Husbands and wives went to the cinema together, a novelty at any rate for the poorer classes. What effect did the cinema have on mankind? Did it make men more truly the masses? Did it stimulate their imaginations to wilder flights? Did it lead them to expect, or even to demand, more dramatic happenings in the world? We have no means of knowing. Observers, themselves usually of a puritanical cast, opined that romantic films provoked sexual activities among the audiences. This, too, was mere speculation.

81 The little man. Charlie Chaplin in *The Gold Rush*

Radio and cinema had one novelty in common: they were forms of communication which dispensed with the written word, except for the captions in silent films. The written word had gone hand in hand with civilization from the beginning. Now, theoretically, an illiterate could be as well-informed about the world as the best-read man. Reading might have been expected to decline as a result, but this did not happen. Perhaps the habit was too inbred. Besides, primary education, now almost universal in Europe, made literacy also universal. Far from declining, the written, or rather the printed word triumphed as never before. Newspapers, which had greatly increased their circulation during the First World War, continued to do so after it. In Great Britain, which carried the process furthest, the Press by 1930 ranked twelfth among British industries, ahead of shipbuilding. Newspapers now counted their readers by millions where they had previously counted by thousands. They had bigger headlines, shorter paragraphs, simpler writing. They derived their incomes mainly from advertisements, not from the halfpennies or pennies paid by readers. The decisive figure was the proprietor – Northcliffe and Beaverbrook in Great Britain, Hugenberg in Germany – not the editor. Nearly all the great newspapers were conservative in character, and often Conservative in allegiance. They were among the most materialistic elements in a materialistic age. Nevertheless, they provided more news than had been provided by even the most esteemed newspapers of a staider past.

82 The latest in cinema architecture. Interior of the Granada in Tooting, London, built in September 1931

83 The leading British Press figure between the wars, Lord Beaverbrook

The newspapers, like the cinema and usually the radio, expressed popular culture, and observers talked as though this were the only culture which now existed. The flood of the mass-age was supposed to have submerged the standards of previous times, but this was far from being the case. There was also a middle culture and a high culture – the distinctions between them resting on levels of sophistication (middlebrow and highbrow), not on class. The middlebrow culture was the least interesting, a repetition of past patterns interspersed with lamentations against anything new, either above or below. Those who condemned James Joyce or Picasso also disapproved of the cinema. These middlebrows felt more menaced than before, hence the intolerance which contrasted oddly with their professions of liberalism. Original artists and thinkers were constantly, though ineffectually, harassed. The works of three great British writers – Joyce, D.H. Lawrence, T.E. Lawrence – came under the legal ban of pornography. The organizer of an art exhibition learned to expect, in England, a visit from the police. In Paris and Berlin he took precautions against a riot.

ENGLISH MODERNS

84, 85, 86, 87 D.H. Lawrence, the coal-miner's son (left), was best known as a novelist, but when his paintings were shown in 1928 (opposite), the police arrived and confiscated them. Aldous Huxley (below left), wrote sophisticated, 'modern' dissections of Society. T.E. Lawrence (below right), hero of the desert war and author of *Seven Pillars of Wisdom*, became a myth in his own time

88, 89, 90 Sylvia Beach and James Joyce in Miss Beach's bookshop (above). Gertrude Stein (right, portrait by Picasso) was in the vanguard of literary experimentation. It was she who characterized Ernest Hemingway (left) as 'false hair on the chest'

Nevertheless, this was an age of intellectual and artistic activity. Paris reached perhaps its highest point as the cultural capital of Europe. English artists had always congregated there, though fewer Germans did so as a result of the First World War. There were now also more Russians, usually refugees for political reasons, and more Americans. These Americans were no longer in Paris merely to learn and to admire; they were there to lead and to create. Ernest Hemingway and Gertrude Stein, for example, counted as decisive figures in European literature. Gertrude Stein was significant in another way. Her writings expressed the spirit of subversion which now shaped much of European art. Many forces combined to end the reign of reason which had run since the Renaissance. In the nineteenth century, for instance, science had powerfully supported rationalistic philosophy. Scientists were expected to discover general laws of increasing certainty, and they expected it themselves. In the twentieth century, scientists began to doubt the finality of their own conclusions, just when ordinary men came to believe that reason had triumphed.

Einstein demonstrated the inadequacy of the Newtonian system. Where the previous result of science had been Positivism, Einstein offered Relativity, an ever-shifting system of truth according to the angle of vision. Physicists similarly shattered the finality of the atom. Scientists cheerfully announced that they did not know what they were doing: 'indeterminacy' was now their basic principle. Most of them pushed resolutely into the unknown, without contemplating the ultimate harvest of destruction which they were preparing for mankind. Einstein was almost alone in coming to regret what he had done; he declared at the end of his life that he would advise a young man to become a plumber.

Scientists challenged reason by implication; others did so directly. Marxism already implied this challenge when it laid down that systems of thought sprang from the existing social order and class allegiance, not from abstract reasoning. Standards of right and wrong were thus, it seemed, relative, like the Universe, and a Soviet statesman could commit crimes which were deplorable elsewhere. Psychology reinforced this outlook. Freud discovered the unconscious and taught that a man's apparently rational acts were in fact often determined by what happened to him before the age of five. In Freud's view, ostensible motives were no more than rationalizations. The real driving forces bubbled up from the storms of the unconscious, to be either sublimated or repressed when they reached the threshold of consciousness. No doubt most men did not grasp the complexities of Freud's system, still less that of the rival psychologist, Jung, who actually postulated a collective unconscious and a folk-memory going back for centuries. In any case, these systems were literary fantasies, not scientific structures; vulgarized, they struck an immense blow against reason.

91, 92, 93 Prophets of the new thought. Sigmund Freud (above), and C.G. Jung (above right), altered basic concepts of mind, behaviour and conscience. Albert Einstein (right), made the most revolutionary discovery in physics of the first half of the twentieth century. The 'theory of relativity' and 'psychoanalysis', aside from their contributions to mankind, became widely bandied clichés

94, 95 Surrealism, an art phenomenon of the late 'twenties. Dali's *Apparition of a face and fruit dish on a beach* (above) and Max Ernst's *Fruit of a long experience* (right) ▶

Philosophers themselves gave up the search for truth. On the Continent, they invented existentialism, an outlook best expressed by the dramatist Pirandello in the title of one of his plays: *It's True If You Think It Is.* Many English philosophers also accepted the view that morality was now a matter of taste and, being nurtured in a more practical tradition than their Continental colleagues, confined themselves to analysing the meaning of words. Value-judgments ceased to have value. Of course, all this had very little effect on real life. Most men, including even philosophers, went on behaving in a moral way. They lived quiet, monogamous lives; were kind to children and animals; and even did their duty as citizens. The old moral sanctions may have lost their force, but men still conformed

to standards, the validity of which they no longer recognized. Indeed the standards were higher than they had been before.

Art and literature reflected the confusions of a relativist age. Technical developments increased the confusion. The classical outlook had long been running down. Painters were no longer concerned to represent faithfully a nature, which in any case they were now taught did not exist. The great school of French Impressionists had already practised the doctrine that the painter's impression was more important than the object which he depicted. In that case, why remain tied to the object at all? The Cubists were concerned with forms which they themselves devised. The Surrealists, as their name implied,

96, 97, 98, 99 Arnold Schoenberg, painted by Egon Schiele in 1917; Alban Berg, painted

escaped from reality and also from reason. Picasso was the acknowledged master of the age, moving rapidly from one manner to another in an attempt to express the dilemma of modern man. Traditional art had been grand and solemn; the new artists brought in humour. They were not ashamed to be funny – an acknowledgment, at any rate, of one human emotion. Every great artist of the twentieth century had in him something of the clown. This bewildered ordinary men, who had been taught to regard art with an almost religious veneration.

Music showed the same decline of old standards and the same search for new ones. Schoenberg, Berg, and Webern abandoned the diatonic scale for the twelve-note row, a form of music which could be comprehended by most people only on the printed page. Other composers sought inspiration in the modes of folk-music. Of these Bartók was the most important, and Vaughan Williams the most English. The most powerful new impulse came from the folk in a

by Schoenberg about 1920; Anton Webern, by Kokoschka; and Bela Bartók

100 Influence on music. Below, Percival Mackey's jazz band rehearsing on a London roof garden

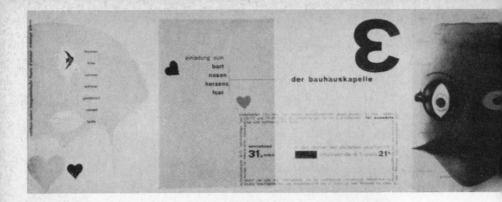

101, 102, 103 Invita-
tion to a *Bauhaus* cos-
tume party, 192.
(above). *Architectur*
by Klee, 1923 (left)
Yellow Accompanimen
by Kandinsky (abov·
right), who left the
Soviet Union in 1922

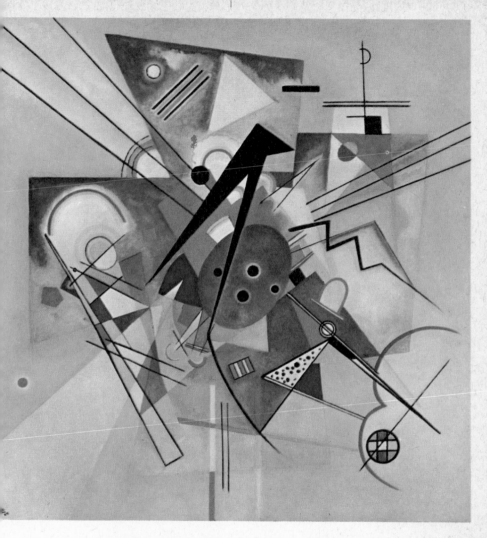

104, 105 Practical objects: a teapot designed by M. Brandt in 1924 and a chair with a frame of nickel-plated steel tubing by Marcel Breuer (1925)

106 The composer Igor Stravinsky, drawn by Picasso

different way: this was jazz or syncopation, which had started in New Orleans before the First World War. Jazz became the universal music for popular dancing and also the main principle of some serious composers. This was remarkable. Of course, Europe had acquired occasional fashions from outside in the past – Chinese follies in the eighteenth century, echoes of Japanese art in the nineteenth. Jazz was more fundamental. Europe, hitherto the universal exporter of culture as of everything else, now imported her musical culture from the African jungle by way of Louisiana. In music also there was a dominating figure, like Picasso in art, who tried everything once: Igor Stravinsky, an expatriate Russian. With exceptional perversity, Stravinsky devoted his revolutionary genius to the service of Christian piety.

107 The *Bauhaus* building in Dessau

Architecture was affected by new techniques as well as new ideas. The modern architect had to build large buildings for communal use – flats, schools, factories, hospitals. His guiding principle was Functionalism: as Le Corbusier put it, 'A house is a machine for living in.' The most significant figure was probably Walter Gropius, who established the *Bauhaus* at Weimar. Modern architecture was more talked about than practised. There were a few modern railway stations in Italy, a few modern blocks of offices in the various capital cities, and many projects of town-planning which never came to fruition; but most houses were still built as though modern systems of building or of heating had never been thought of. They were the triumph of custom over reason – perhaps also, therefore, symbolic of their age.

108 Luigi Pirandello

109 André Gide

110 T.S. Eliot

111 Marcel Proust

The writers were still more destructive. They destroyed both form and ideas. The poets abandoned rhyme and metre for free verse – stretches of prose chopped arbitrarily into lengths. T.S. Eliot was the most successful of them, and *The Waste Land* spoke for the age even in its title. In France, poets abandoned even words, and the Dada school wrote instead in grunts. The writers of prose took a similar course. Marcel Proust destroyed the traditional framework of time. James Joyce went further and tried to destroy the English language. André Gide announced that an act had value only if it were gratuitous, that is, devoid of all human significance. The realist theatre of Ibsen and Shaw fell out of fashion; in its place came Expressionism – little scenery, less sense, and much violence. Berlin was the centre of this school, with Georg Kaiser as its most effective exponent. After him came Bertolt Brecht, who brought the class war on to the stage, with the assistance of Kurt Weill's music. The cultural importance of Berlin was new and striking; for a number of years it seemed more alive and up-to-date than Paris, and adventurous spirits found a home there.

112, 113 Berlin Expressionists, Kurt Weill and Bertolt Brecht

114 'Man is Man', a Berliner Ensemble production of Brecht's play

Yet it was not all gloom, disillusion, and destruction. There was also a good deal of fun. It was difficult to take Salvador Dali altogether seriously when he attempted to address an audience from within a diver's helmet. English was especially rich in comic genius – P.G. Wodehouse the more popular, Evelyn Waugh the more sophisticated. Rather oddly, the defunct Austrian empire did best of all: it produced the two comic masterpieces of the age. Laughter from them reverberates down the years. *The Good Soldier Schweik* by a Czech, Jaroslav Hašek, recorded the triumphs of an ordinary man over the upheavals of war, and *The Confessions of Zeno*, by Italo Svevo, an inhabitant of Trieste, rose high above the confusions of existence. It was fortunate that some writers appeared who did not take the age too seriously.

Ordinary people were indeed bewildered when they tried to understand what the creative artists were doing. 'Alienation' worked both ways. Artists might pride themselves on rising above popular taste, but the people responded by not taking much notice of the artists. In mundane affairs there seemed much ground for cheerfulness. Europe had seemingly been restored to her old position of predominance in the world. India was settling down to the slow march of ordered liberty under the benevolent direction of Lord Irwin, later Earl Halifax – a process which, according to all precedent, would take some centuries. China had become a national state on the European pattern, its democracy secured in theory by Chiang Kai-Shek. In return, China presented Europe with the new leisure uniform of jeans. The countries of the Middle East were also supposed to be taking the first steps towards European constitutionalism. In 1927, Trotsky, the apostle of international revolution, was finally thrust from power and position – a sign, apparently, that Soviet Russia was also becoming a respectable, conservative state. In the same year, Europeans displayed their renewed independence of the United States by demonstrations in favour of Sacco and Vanzetti, two anarchists who, it was said, had been framed by American justice.

The authority of the League of Nations was respected by every country except Soviet Russia, and even the Bolsheviks had ceased to believe that the League was the heart of a capitalist conspiracy against them. Geneva had become the political centre of the world. In 1928, at the time of the Kellogg Pact, by which every signatory country renounced war as a means of policy, the First World War seemed far away. There was an outburst of war books in England and Germany, with *All Quiet on the Western Front* the most famous. All sang the same tune: the horror and futility of war, the confidence that there would never be another. 'No More War' was a refrain in every language. Hope knew no limits. Space, nature, poverty had been conquered. As Ramsay MacDonald announced, 'up and up and up, and on and on and on'. Men were confident that great things were going to happen, and they were confident that these great things would be uniformly agreeable. The year 1929 seemed to represent the peak of human achievement. It was in fact the watershed: ten years after the end of the First World War, ten years before the outbreak of the second.

The Great Depression was the central event in inter-war Europe, as memorable and decisive in its way as the French Revolution or the First World War. The onset of the Depression can be precisely dated. American stock markets had prospered almost uninterruptedly since 1921 and had boomed fantastically for eighteen months. On 24 October 1929 the boom burst; share prices fell even faster than they had risen, and thousands of speculators were ruined. The American financial crash soon hit Europe. American loans to Europe had already stopped; now American purchases from Europe stopped also. The European economy was precariously balanced. Recovery had brought a great increase in productive powers, with little corresponding increase in markets. Prosperity had been maintained by the flood of American dollars. Now European factories, too, closed their gates. Within two years, world trade was more than halved. Unemployment soared, particularly in the more industrialized countries. There were over two million unemployed in Great Britain; four million, then six million, in Germany.

European economy had been punctuated by similar depressions throughout the nineteenth century, but the Great Depression was more savage than its predecessors. It lasted longer: the first signs of recovery did not appear until the autumn of 1932. It was world wide. It hit the producers of foodstuffs and raw materials even harder than the industrial countries. Nowhere in the world were consumers waiting with purchases which would begin the process of recovery. Moreover, the Great Depression hit all classes. Previously it was those directly dependent on industry, capitalists and workers, who had felt the main impact of a crisis, while those living on fixed incomes had actually benefited as prices fell. Now salaries, particularly state salaries, were cut even more sharply than wages. In some countries, holders of state bonds had already lost their savings during the

◀ 115 The martyrs. *The Passion of Sacco and Vanzetti* by Ben Shahn (1931–32)

inflation; in others, the interest on the bonds was reduced. The staid middle class, which had been the most stable element in society, was now threatened with the fate of a white-collared proletariat. It was driven towards resentment, if not towards revolution, and society lost its sheet-anchor of middle-class respectability.

When an individual businessman cannot sell his goods, he either goes bankrupt or reduces his prices – probably both. The public authorities, statesmen and bankers alike, knew no other way of meeting the Depression on a national scale. They could not go bankrupt; therefore the only answer was that prices must come down. Public expenditure and wages were reduced. In some countries, such as Germany, prices themselves were directly reduced by government action. Each step in this policy made the Depression worse: still fewer consumers than before, or rather, still fewer consumers who could afford to buy. There was another instinctive response. It seemed obvious that the dwindling market, such as it was, should be reserved for the producers of each individual country. Tariffs were pushed up in every European state, and in 1932 Great Britain, the last champion of Free Trade, went over to Protection. Breaches of the old liberal system went further. Quotas, cartels, export bounties ravaged international trade. In 1931 Great Britain abandoned the gold standard after an ineffectual attempt to defend it, mainly at the expense of the unemployed. Throughout the 1930s, the pound sterling was a managed currency, its international value deliberately held down in order to benefit British exporters.

Germany broke even more decisively with international principles and loyalties. In 1924, after the inflation, the German mark had also acquired a gold parity, and the Germans, too, worshipped the Golden Calf in theory. Actually, the altar was empty: Germany had no gold and few international reserves. Since memories of the inflation prevented any retreat from parity, the theoretical value of the mark was maintained by legal force. Germans were forbidden to buy foreign currencies. Foreign traders and bondholders had to accept blocked marks, which could be spent only in Germany at a depreciated rate. Most foreign trade was conducted by barter, and Germany's creditors took goods which they did not want rather than receive nothing at all. Currency control turned Germany into a police state long before Hitler established his dictatorship. Letters were opened; private accounts were scrutinized; travellers were searched for currency at the frontiers. The siege economy of wartime was restored, when Europe was still ostensibly at peace.

The principles of economic liberalism were abandoned, for the most part, unwillingly – indeed, to the accompaniment of ringing declarations that the abandonment was only temporary. Nearly all the experts were agreed that the Depression had been caused by interferences with the natural laws of economics, such as tariffs and 'doles' to the unemployed. At international conferences, statesmen promised to return to Free Trade as soon as circumstances allowed them to do so; after each such promise, tariffs and restrictions mounted higher. The economists were caught in a hopeless dilemma. For generations past, they had extolled the virtues of *laissez-faire*, proclaiming that all would be well if every man pursued his own economic interest. Thus left to himself, the ordinary man pursued his interest by combining with others – the employer in cartels, the worker in trade unions. *Laissez-faire* could not be maintained by leaving things alone; there had to be constant attempts to prevent what was in fact the natural course, and such attempts were difficult, if not impossible, in democratic communities. The free economy, far from working of itself, had become a most unnatural order.

A few thinkers stumbled towards the idea that it would be better to make a virtue of planning, instead of watching its advent with lamentation. Lloyd George, who had been ready to direct economic life in wartime, offered himself unavailingly once again. Within the ranks of the British Labour Party, Sir Oswald Mosley devised the full programme of a planned economy. His reward was to be rejected with ignominy by the Labour Party. Planning was not only alarming in itself, as a conscious repudiation of previous teachings; it ran up against the problem: planning for what purpose? Planning in wartime had been simple: its object had been to win the war. But what should be its object in peacetime? Since most European states were now supposed to be serving the needs of the masses, it might be supposed that there would be a simple answer: planning should

116 Labour victor at Smethwick. Sir Oswald Mosley, returned to Parliament in 1929, later became the leading British Fascist

promote general prosperity. But, while the communities had become politically democratic, they had remained dictatorships in economic affairs. The rich men who conducted these affairs – bankers, capitalists, and industrialists – did not welcome plans which would carry through a social revolution or even diminish their riches. The national appeal had been effective only in wartime, and now every attempt at planning brought with it a return to war-psychology. In this way war grew unconsciously out of the Depression.

The most extraordinary feature of the Great Depression was that it brought no benefit to the Socialist and Communist parties. The capitalist system seemed to be breaking down, exactly as Marx had foretold. Here was the final crisis which the faithful had been waiting for since the middle of the nineteenth century. There were many manifestations of discontent – street riots in Germany, hunger marches by the unemployed in Great Britain – but there was no Socialist revolution in any European country, and Socialist parties rarely increased their votes even in free elections. Spain was the only country where Socialists came within sight of success, and this was for old-fashioned nineteenth-century reasons which had nothing to do with the Great Depression. The moderate Socialist parties had, no doubt, long ceased to have any real belief in revolution. They were usually closely associated with the trade unions, and these were ravaged by the Depression. Besides, the unions owed their very existence to the capitalist system and were concerned to get it going again. Unions, after all, had no purpose unless there were bosses to negotiate with. Moreover, the employed workers kept up their standards fairly well even in the worst times. The strongest resentment was felt by the unemployed and by the unorganized middle class: a resentment which turned as much against the unions as against the rich, or perhaps more so.

The Communists had apparently more advantages. They were not identified with the present system. On the contrary, they represented in theory the cause of revolution against it. In practice they, too, had a settled place in society. The leaders of the Communist Party were office-workers like any other bureaucrats. They had neither qualification nor wish to man the barricades. Perhaps revolutionary tunes were less effective when played the second time round. The Communists had had their moment of opportunity after the First World War; now they seemed as outmoded as anyone else.

117 The first hunger-marchers, London, 1932

Socialism, even in its Communist form, was old-fashioned in a deeper sense. The advance into Socialism, according to Marx, was to be a last triumph of *laissez-faire*. Socialism would grow out of events, just as capitalism had done before it. The strength of the existing states would be weakened and finally destroyed by capitalism's failure, so that the Socialist revolution would be easy, almost unnoticed. Instead, the Great Depression made the organs of the state stronger. The state interfered more; the police became more violent; the discontented became more cowed. Even the hunger marches were demonstrations for relief within the existing system, not demands for its overthrow. There was never a time when Socialist revolution was less likely, or less possible, than at the height of the Great Depression.

The paradox of Socialist failure went further. Just at the time when the old outcome of revolution proved barren, the rulers of Soviet Russia stumbled on the new answer of Planning, which non-Socialist countries were also giving, equally without prevision. The writings of Marx had not a word about a planned economy; indeed, Marx always insisted that Socialism would run itself totally without direction, exactly as depicted in *News from Nowhere*. Even Lenin waited on events once he had seized power. It did not occur to him that Socialism was possible in a single country. Lenin died in 1924, still waiting. Thereafter, the events for which the Bolsheviks waited took an alarming turn from their point of view. Capitalism recovered throughout Europe and threatened to revive even within Russia itself. In 1927 Bukharin, the leading Soviet theorist, addressed to the Russian peasants the very exhortation which Guizot had once addressed to the French *bourgeoisie*: 'Get rich.' If the Bolsheviks waited much longer, a new revolution might well happen – but inside Russia in favour of capitalism, not outside Russia against it. Fumblingly and without seeming to realize the full extent of their heresy, the Communist rulers of Russia determined to go against events instead of waiting for them.

Stalin was the spokesman of this new course. In later years he was to be accused, no doubt rightly, of a ruthless appetite for personal power; but this was not the cause of his original success. His strength, compared to the other Bolsheviks, lay in his practical nature. He was a stolid, competent administrator, with little grasp of theory. Where others were enmeshed in Marxist dogmas, Stalin saw only that these dogmas were leading to disaster. If Russia was not moving towards Socialism naturally, was indeed moving away from it, then she must be forced into Socialism unnaturally by interference from above. Marxism was stood on its head. The Master had taught that the economic system of the time determined the political superstructure. Now the political superstructure was going to impose a new economic system. The arguments were not put in a clear-cut way. Stalin and his supporters claimed to be orthodox Marxists, and relied on the simple equation that, since they were Communists, anything they did was obviously in line with historical development. Stalin's opponents, with equal perversity, accused him of betraying Socialism in the interests of the bureaucracy. By 1928 the decision was made: Soviet Russia embarked on the first Five-Year Plan.

The decision had wide consequences both for Soviet Russia and for European civilization. A planned economy, particularly when it was designed to promote heavy industry in a backward agrarian country, inevitably meant a revival of dictatorial rule. The problem of 'primitive accumulation', to which Marx had devoted much attention, was solved by the simple device of keeping the mass of the population at starvation level. The Russian peasants did not care for this solution: when the towns failed to produce consumer goods, they retaliated by cutting down their production of food. Stalin and the Communist state seized food supplies for the towns by force; the more recalcitrant peasants were slaughtered or driven to Siberia. There was a new civil war, more terrible than the civil war which had accompanied the Bolshevik revolution, and more terrible than the Second World War, according to Stalin himself. Nobody knows how many Russians perished: some millions, perhaps three, perhaps six. Ultimately the peasants were cowed, the civil war, in a sense, won. The victory, however, was only relative. The dictatorship and the terror could not be relaxed. The Communists had always repudiated *bourgeois* ideas of tolerance and freedom. But only the planned economy identified Communism with the knock of the secret police on the door, the anonymous informant, and the labour camp. As often happens when men have strayed, the Communists then made a virtue of their crimes. Acceptance of them became a shibboleth for the faithful.

Stalinist planning achieved its object, though no doubt in an extremely wasteful way. The economic strength of Soviet Russia was pushed up by these artificial means. At the outbreak of the First World War, the Russian empire had occupied a humble place among the Great Powers from an economic point of view: securely ahead of Italy, but doubtfully ahead of any other except perhaps Austria-Hungary. At the start of the Second World War, Russia was still behind the United States, but she was running neck-and-neck with Germany for second place. This gigantic transformation was Stalin's doing – perhaps the greatest interference with events by any individual in European history. Certainly, compared with Stalin, Peter the Great was a village blacksmith. Of course Stalin acted through the Communist bureaucracy and spoke on their behalf. He was distinguished by his will, not by vision or intelligence. This will raised Soviet Russia to the rank of a World Power; its effect was perhaps all the greater because of the lack of foresight which accompanied it.

The Stalinist plans also changed Soviet Russia's place in Europe. They made her both more remote and more active, or, at any rate, more capable of action. In the 1920s foreign observers judged, rightly, that Soviet Russia had little strength for foreign affairs, except in her ideological appeal. The Comintern was as important to Russia's security as the Red Army. In the following decade, foreign observers wrote Soviet Russia off even more than during the tyranny and the confusions of the five-year plans. A few of these observers predicted, however, that Russia would emerge from her torments as the greatest of European powers. Again both observations were broadly right: Russia was both actually weak and potentially strong. Those who hesitated to involve Soviet Russia in European affairs could never decide whether her aid was not worth having or whether she would gobble up those whom she professed to aid. In either case, Soviet Russia was much more of an enigma to Europe than she had been in the 1920s.

118 Mature Bolshevik art. *Denikinites fleeing from Novorossiisk*, by Vladimirsky

The standing of international Communism changed along with Russia's. The Comintern and its dependent parties had been exploited almost from the beginning for Soviet Russia's protection. European Communists were expected to hamper the alleged plans for a counter-revolutionary war and, at the very least, to encourage trade with Soviet Russia on favourable terms. But there were mutual advantages. The Soviet authorities helped the other Communist parties lavishly with finance, and the Russian members of the Comintern did not yet claim that they had discovered the ideal way of doing things. Until 1928 the Russians still admitted that theirs was a backward country and that an effective Socialist community must wait for revolution elsewhere. With the five-year plan, the Russian Communists claimed to be building a perfect society, virtually without assistance. The blunders and follies in their makeshift planning were presented as essential features of Socialism. Moreover, the five-year plan was implicitly a nationalistic venture. It asserted that Socialism was possible in a single country; and from this, it was an easy step to assert that it was not possible otherwise. A Communist revolution outside Russia would have thrown out the planning figures and thus retarded the five-year plan. The Comintern, which had not been strikingly successful in promoting revolutions, now became an active agent in preventing them. Not that its activity amounted to much. Socialism in one country removed its mainspring. Though it remained nominally alive throughout the 1930s, few noticed the difference when Stalin ordered its dissolution in 1943.

European Communism was not solely a manufacture of the Comintern. It sprang from natural discontent and rested on European traditions. Here, too, the five-year plans brought about changes. Soviet Russia of the 1920s could be presented as a symbol of rebellion and defiance against the established order. A decade later, she had herself become a symbol of order, even if order of a slightly different sort. Graphs of planned economy were now more significant than the Red flag. The foreign admirers of Soviet Russia admired for new reasons. Workers, however discontented and impoverished, were not much moved by the call of planning. Even a quite thick-headed worker appreciated that, whoever benefited from planning, he would not. On the contrary, industrial conscription was the first requirement of a planned economy, in Soviet Russia as elsewhere. This objection did not occur to middle-class enthusiasts for planning, who in any case would be planning others, not being ordered about themselves. Hence, working-class admiration for Soviet Russia ran down or, at any rate, went flat. Instead there grew a middle-class craze for Soviet Russia, far blinder and more unquestioning than the older admiration had been. It took a good deal of infatuation to announce that Soviet Russia had discovered the secret of a perfect society in, say, 1932, when some million Russian peasants were dying of famine. But the middle-class planners, undaunted, took it in their stride. The plans went wrong; the figures were fantasies when they were not forged; the terror grew stricter; the hostility towards foreigners became greater. Still the chorus of academic admiration swelled.

This gave the culture of the 1930s a most peculiar twist. Marxists of all schools agreed that the middle classes must be destroyed, violently or otherwise, and that the working class must reign in their stead. Now the workers were by no means warm towards the Communist cause, and distinguished members of the middle class were clamouring for their own destruction. The paradoxical situation reached its extreme in the United States, where more Communists were to be found in the State Department than in the Ford automobile works, if anyone had looked for them. A similar contrast existed in European countries, particularly in those where the intellectuals were free to call their own tunes. The literary or intellectual rebel of the past had been a rebel against everything, to the best of his ability. In this strange decade, he became a rebel for conformity and order, lamenting that his lot had fallen in easy places. The most devout paraded their conviction – flattering but incorrect – that they would be the first to be liquidated in the event of a Communist revolution, and continued to advocate this revolution all the same.

These paradoxes contained some sense. It had been accepted, ever since the First World War, that Communism was the only alternative to capitalist democracy, and, with the latter breaking down, conversion to Communism seemed an obvious intellectual course. However, the expectations of the political pundits and historians, as usual, did not work out. A third runner appeared and, for a time, threatened to scoop the pool. The 1930s were not dominated by the conflict between Communism and democracy, though according to the rules they should have been. Fascism was the special feature of the decade, though again the experts were wrong about it. They expected Fascism to last for many years; instead it proved one of the most transient episodes in European civilization, however unpleasant while it lasted.

Fascism in its traditional, that is to say, its Italian form had nothing to offer against the Great Depression. Though some intellectuals had shown their cleverness by cracking up Fascism as an improvement on capitalism, when the Great Depression broke Mussolini was as lacking in resource as any democratic statesman. Italy had the same troubles as France or any other democratic state: unemployment, declining production, and general stagnation. Mussolini applied the normal capitalist remedies. He maintained the currency, reduced government expenditure, and lamented the growth of nationalistic economics.

The new form of Fascism appeared in Germany and owed its character partly to the moment of its triumph. German Fascism, unlike Mussolini's, came to power in the Great Depression and therefore had to do something about it. This German Fascism was not new; like the original Italian article, it had begun after the First World War, as an outburst of national pride and resentment against defeat. It was, in the strictest sense, a movement of reaction. It was against everything which had happened in 1919 – against the system of the victors, as much against the League of Nations as against reparations. It was equally opposed to the system of the Weimar republic – against democracy, particularly Social Democracy, and against all the ideas of western liberalism. The roots of National Socialism went far back into German history. Some German thinkers, from Fichte if not from Luther, had always repudiated western ideas as being both foreign and liberal. They had preached the innate mystical superiority of the German race, and racialism was an essential part of National Socialism. Even though National Socialism had clear antecedents, it needed the resentments of the post-war years to give it force, particularly when monetary inflation added the resentment of the lower middle class to that of the defeated. National Socialism rested on all those who had no secure place in society. Its rallying cry, to quote the title of a popular novel, was *Little Man, What Now?* To the disgruntled and feckless, it offered the glamour of parades in quasi-military uniform and the promise of power for some undefined purpose of destruction.

Though National Socialism was revolutionary in spirit if not in policy, it appealed also to two classes normally on the side of order: the military leaders and the capitalists. The military leaders wished to shake off the heritage of defeat. In practical terms, they wanted to end German disarmament and, more vaguely, they looked forward to a new war, bringing the victory which they thought ought to have been theirs in 1918. The capitalists resented the increased power of the trade unions and feared the further encroachments of welfare in a democratic society. Both capitalists and generals were lured by

119 Nazis in the making. Children demonstrating in Munich in 1925

the prospects which National Socialism held out to them, despite the dislike they sometimes felt for its barbarous methods. The professional middle class of lawyers and civil servants took up a more equivocal attitude. They held strongly to the rule of law, which had long been the pride of Germans, but, on the other hand, they hankered after the vanished imperial society and would not be reconciled to the new democracy. They acquiesced reluctantly in the march of National Socialism. Though they were often ashamed of what they were doing, they acquiesced all the same.

Most societies have an underworld of crackpots and layabouts. German National Socialism was transformed into a mighty force by a single man, its Leader, Adolf Hitler. He was the Unknown Soldier, the little man of Chaplin's inspiration, come to life and turned sour.

120 Hitler the Bavarian—in Landsberg prison with Hess (fourth from left) and other friends

His mind was a junk-store of tired, second-hand ideas, which he revived by his intense belief in them. He picked up and intensified a doctrine, common at the time, that Germany had been betrayed, when on the point of victory, by the 'November criminals' – that is, by the Social Democrats and others who had concluded the armistice. Hence there followed a simple political deduction: if the democratic politicians and the democratic system were overthrown, Germany would again become great and powerful. Revolutionaries have always promised great things. None did so more plausibly than Hitler, or with such primitive means.

In domestic affairs, Hitler had no programme except action, and this was mostly destructive. In foreign affairs also his programme was destructive: an end to the international system created by the peacemakers of 1919. This was no mere revision of grievances and defects. Europe, which existed on the basis that Germany had lost the war, was to be rearranged on the basis that she had won. Hitler claimed further to have a creative purpose in his plans of conquest.

132

The Germans were to find in eastern Europe the living space which the Anglo-Saxon peoples had found in the New World. A German equivalent of the United States would appear in the Ukraine. 'Living space' was a phrase which Hitler had learned from geopolitics. It had no firm significance: Germany did not suffer from over-population. In any case, according to Hitler himself, the main purpose of living space in the Ukraine was to enable Germany to withstand blockade in a future war against Great Britain and France, even though, in his usual contradictory way, he postulated that such a war was unnecessary.

All this rigmarole amounted to little more than a determination to restore and to perpetuate Germany's victories in the First World War. The German General Staff and Bethmann Hollweg, the German Chancellor, had then pursued living space in the east with all Hitler's ambition, even if without the geopolitical trimmings.

21 Hitler the Prussian –
greeting Hindenburg
in front of the
Berlin State Opera
in February 1934

Indeed, Hitler was more moderate than his predecessors, in that he did not aspire to colonies overseas nor to territorial gains in western Europe – though naturally his modesty diminished when the chance of such gains actually matured. Living space itself was the invention of a British geopolitician, Sir Halford Mackinder. Hitler's enthusiasm for the German race echoed the pseudo-scientific racialism common in the later nineteenth century, and was no sillier than E.A. Freeman, Kipling, and Joseph Chamberlain on the Anglo-Saxons or than almost any Frenchman on 'la grande nation'.

Hitler's strongest fanaticism was for anti-Semitism, and this, too, had a long, though no doubt disreputable, intellectual history. Many countries, in their time, had expelled the Jews, as Germany was to do under Hitler; the Inquisition had burned Jews, as again Germany was to do. Racialists in France had deplored the admixture of Jewish blood. In the early twentieth century, Radical Roman Catholics such as Belloc and Chesterton had discovered that the Jews were corrupting British politics. Every fantasy in Hitler's system of ideas had forerunners and parallels elsewhere; the only difference was that Hitler took his ideas literally, and anti-Semitism most literally of all. Where others talked of eliminating Jewish influence from political or cultural life, without any clear idea of what they meant, Hitler saw the answer in precise terms of physical destruction. The First World War had taught people that it was righteous to kill others by the million for the sake of the nation. Hitler carried the doctrine further and held that it was righteous to kill others for the sake of any idea which came into his head. He was the end-product of a civilization of clever talk and helped to shake that civilization by taking the talk seriously.

Few except himself took Hitler seriously in his early days. He arrived too late to profit from the immediate confusions after the First World War. In 1923 he attempted to seize power in Munich on a ticket which combined anti-Communism and extreme nationalism. The attempt failed, and Hitler was imprisoned, under agreeable circumstances. When he emerged from prison, Germany was prosperous, and the Nazis in their brown uniforms were no more than a minor nuisance, irresponsible youngsters playing at politics. There was no social peril from which Hitler could save Germany, as Mussolini had claimed to save Italy. The Communists were an exhausted, harmless force and, while most Germans agreed with Hitler's denunciations of the peace settlement, they also thought that revision could wait for a future generation. Only the Great Depression put the wind into Hitler's sails. Every other party was obviously helpless against it. Hitler held out the promise that he would do something effective, though neither he nor anyone else knew what. Support for the National Socialist Party grew at every general election, of which Germany had many. The more youthful unemployed were glad to find occupation, and even some maintenance, as storm troopers. It was the Salvation Army all over again, this time promising Heaven on earth.

Even so, the existing political order lurched on until 1933. Great Britain, not Germany, was the centre of interest in the first years of the Depression. A political upheaval there in 1931 threatened to destroy the Labour Party, actually destroyed the Liberal Party, and ended the traditional institutions of the gold standard and Free Trade. The year 1931 would do very well as the end of the long Liberal era, were it not that the supposedly new political forces in Great Britain proved to be almost as free-wheeling as the old Liberals. Still, Great Britain seemed to be leading the way towards managed currency and a closed economic system. In Germany, there was only the dreary round of deflation, imposed by emergency decree, which the Reichstag would neither oppose nor support. German governments operated in the void. Hitler and the Nazis did not conquer power; they were intrigued into power by some particularly frivolous members of the old governing class, who imagined that they could take Hitler prisoner. At the end of January 1933, Hitler became Chancellor. Within a month he had destroyed the safeguards of the democratic constitution and was on the way to shaking off all other hindrances to his dictatorship. This was a dictatorship of a peculiar sort: a dictatorship of the masses over themselves. Though the National Socialists did not win a majority of votes at any free general election, they won more votes than any other German party had ever done. A few months after coming to power, they received practically all the votes recorded – an achievement which cannot be credited solely to terrorism, still less to fraud. No dictatorship has been so ardently desired or so firmly supported by so many people as Hitler's was in Germany. Demagogues and revolutionaries had always invoked the masses against the established order. Hitler was the first to whose call the masses responded: the most demagogic, if not the most democratic, statesman there has ever been.

Hitler and the Nazis present the historian with an almost insoluble problem. They are too loathsome to be treated easily with detachment. Criminals, barbarians, or – at the most charitable – madmen, seem the only appropriate descriptions. Yet all such phrases cause misunderstanding. Hitler was not a barbarian like Attila, breaking into a civilized Europe. He, his ideas, and his system were all products of European civilization, however unwelcome this now appears. Some observers explained Hitler by the brutality and militarism of the Germans; and many Germans were brutal and militaristic. Other observers regarded Hitler as a last desperate throw by capitalism; and many German capitalists expected to benefit from Hitler's destruction of the trade unions. A rather shaky, discontented society

122, 123 Nazi art and architecture. *The Third Reich*, a heroic allegory (right) by Richard Klein. Far right, the entrance to the Nuremberg parade-ground, scene of Nazi mass rallies

was pulled into order by the confident promises of a man who believed passionately in himself. Probably no one will make sense of German Fascism in our lifetime. No doubt most Germans did not appreciate at first what they were in for. No doubt many were pulled regretfully along. However, the most evil system of modern times was also the most popular, and it is silly to claim otherwise.

People in other countries were also to make out later that they had been deceived by Hitler and had failed to appreciate his true character. This is a pretence. Hitler was on the whole a frank statesman; the trouble was that others did not believe what he said. When he announced that he proposed to make Germany again the greatest power in Europe, this was taken as the ordinary sort of boasting which any statesman might use when he first came to high office. Besides, the political order in Europe had a single unfailing remedy for unruly demagogues, and this was to tame them by responsibility. This remedy was applied to Hitler, first by the governing classes in Germany and then by the rulers of other countries. Surely he would one day be bewitched by the glitter of respectability. Instead, Hitler exploited the concessions made to him by others and grew more confident with each easy success.

It would be absurd to suggest that all the troubles of the 1930s were caused by Hitler. The civilization of the time was inherently unstable, both throughout Europe and in each country. Mass unemployment and general poverty sapped the old loyalties. Marx's statement that the workers had no country seemed to have come true. Those in power – bankers and industrialists as much as politicians – having lost faith in themselves, existed on sufferance and were grateful if they were allowed to survive. All trembled at the thought of strong or decisive action. The European system of states rested solely on the French army, which proved an ineffective instrument. The French lived under the shadow of their death-roll in the First World War and were determined not to go to war again. Their army, equipped only for defence, could do nothing against Germany, even in the days of German disarmament.

There was no longer anything in the nature of a European Balance of Power. Germany was potentially much stronger than France, as everyone knew, and no other power seemed likely to go to France's assistance. Great Britain had virtually withdrawn from Europe and was concerned to distribute even-handed justice between Germany and France, in so far as she had a European policy at all. Some unworldly diplomatists pursued the fantasy that Italy could be enlisted on the French side, thus disregarding both Italy's weakness and the extreme improbability that one Fascist dictator could be turned against the other. All that remained were the powers outside Europe, and there was little prospect of involving them in European affairs. The United States was in a frenzy of isolationism, reinforced by the Great Depression. Japan was attempting to turn the Far East into her private domain and encroached on European interests there while doing so. Soviet Russia was immersed in the turmoils and mysteries of the five-year plan.

Anti-Bolshevism is said to have played a considerable part in the policy of the so-called democratic powers. British and French capitalists, if not British and French statesmen, are alleged to have welcomed Hitler as the saviour of Germany from Communism and as the protector of Europe from Soviet Communism – perhaps even as leader of an anti-Bolshevik crusade at some time in the future. It

124 Victim of collective security. Haile Selassie, King of Abyssinia, addresses the League of Nations in 1936

is doubtful whether any English or French leaders applied their minds so ruthlessly or so clearly. They were no doubt relieved when Hitler provided a stable government in Germany after the previous confusions. With ingenious perversity, they regarded Soviet Russia as both weak and dangerous – on either count undesirable as an ally and probably unattainable as well. This was as far as they got. There had been a power vacuum in eastern Europe ever since the Bolshevik revolution, and western statesmen were content that it should remain a vacuum. In this uneasy state, they contemplated with puzzled dismay the prospect that Germany would inevitably grow stronger and, under Hitler, probably more troublesome as well.

The system of 1919 fell to pieces almost without Hitler's pushing against it. General disarmament had long been the security which western statesmen had in mind. A World Disarmament Conference met in 1932 and immediately reached a deadlock which was never broken. Two years later the conference separated in failure and conflict. This disintegration was completed in 1935 when the League of Nations also showed its helplessness to the world. Mussolini, in search of glory and colonies, attacked Abyssinia, a member of the League of Nations. Fifty-two nations put Italy under ban, mobilized sanctions against her, brandished the formidable threat of collective security. The only result of this display was that the Emperor of Ethiopia lost all his kingdom, instead of losing half, as Mussolini had originally intended. The inhabitants of Abyssinia had some five years of civilized rule until the British, in the Second World War, put the Emperor back again. The short-lived Italian conquest of Abyssinia marked, unexpectedly, the end of an era in European affairs: it was the last acquisition of colonial territory by a European power. Soon the tide would be running the other way: expulsion and surrender, not conquest. The Italians were the last to acquire empire and the first to lose it. They were soon followed by the Dutch, the French, the British, and the Belgians.

Ever since 1919 men had been saying, 'Unless there is general disarmament, unless the League of Nations proves effective, there will be another great war.' Now the attempts at disarmament had broken down, and the League of Nations had broken down too. From that moment, there was a feeling in men's minds that the guns would somehow go off of themselves. In every country the chiefs of staff urgently demanded rearmament, and they did so with an assumption that war was inevitable. Rearmament was greatest in Germany, if only because she had started at the bottom of the ladder. It was less than others alleged and than Hitler himself boasted. Germany's economic recovery, which was complete by 1936, did not rest on rearmament; it was caused mainly by lavish expenditure on public works, particularly on motor roads, and this public spending stimulated private spending also, as Keynes had said it would. Hitler actually skimped on armaments, despite his boasting, partly because he wished to avoid the unpopularity which a reduction of the German standard of living would cause, but more from the confident belief that he would always succeed by bluff. Thus, paradoxically, while nearly everyone else in Europe expected a great war, Hitler was the one man who neither expected nor planned for it.

Men regarded war as inevitable in itself. They also tried to discover rational causes, if any causes of war can ever be dignified with that name. There was the desire of the disgruntled powers, Germany and Italy, to reassert their greatness. They were supposed, also, to be 'have-not' powers, and reputedly intelligent men even imagined that they would be satisfied if they were given equal access to raw materials in some undefined way. Germany had more practical grievances against the peace settlement in the shape of German minorities in Czechoslovakia and Poland. Hitler found his greatest grievance in lack of 'living space', a concept usefully undefined, which enabled him to remain permanently aggrieved. There was also a deep ideological conflict which strengthened the belief in war's inevitability. Fascism was not the only outstanding feature of European civilization in the 1930s. Anti-Fascism was the other, an outlook devised partly by the Communists and partly by men of genuinely democratic mind. Ideological hostility towards Mussolini had come almost entirely from the Socialist parties of Europe. Few middle-class intellectuals, for instance, refrained from visiting Italy merely because Mussolini was in power. Hostility towards Hitler was as much a middle-class as a working-class cause.

Men of goodwill had expected more from Germany than from Italy, which had always been a rough, turbulent country – the breeding-ground of Anarchists before it became the breeding-ground of Fascism. Germany had been, in many ways, the model country of contemporary civilization. Her scientists led the world. New architecture originated largely from the *Bauhaus*. New theatre originated largely from Max Reinhardt and the Expressionists. Germany had the most perfect of democratic constitutions and the strongest Social Democratic party. No other country announced more often that it was a *Rechtstaat* – a country where law ruled. The best foreign correspondents of the day chose Berlin as their centre, thinking rightly that it was the most interesting and exciting European city to be in. Many people in other countries were ashamed of the things which they and, still more, others had said about Germany during the First World War, and bounced back exaggeratedly in the opposite direction.

125, 126 Civilization
fire. The burning of
Reichstag in Febru
1933 (left), and N
students in Berlin burr
books offensive to t
ideology

Deutsche Studenten
wider den
undeutschen Geist

Suddenly, all the worst things which had been said about Germany seemed to be proved true. Hitler was no sooner in power than he abolished democratic safeguards. Freedom of the press ceased to exist; all political parties except the National Socialist ceased to exist; the churches were threatened. Hitler's opponents were imprisoned in concentration camps without trial. These things were not happening in some remote Asiatic state. They were not cloaked in secrecy, as the terror was in Soviet Russia, but happened at the centre of civilization and before the eyes of the world. A month after Hitler became Chancellor, the debating chamber of the Reichstag went up in flames. Hitler announced that this was the work of Communist conspirators, and his opponents alleged that the Reichstag had been fired by the Nazis themselves. The affair became the most famous legal 'case' of the twentieth century. There was a trial before the Supreme Court at Leipzig, where the Bulgarian, Dimitrov, later head of the Comintern, became the hero of democratic Europe. There was also a counter-trial in London, engineered by Communists behind the scenes, which triumphantly demonstrated the guilt of the Nazis. After all this turmoil, it is drab to have to record that the burning of the Reichstag, according to the evidence, was the individual work of a Dutchman, Van der Lubbe, who was neither a Communist nor a Nazi agent; he was merely a human being who disliked the Nazis.

127 The noble Aryan race. Nazis picket Jewish-owned shops in Germany

Hitler's worst offence, in the eyes of Europe, was anti-Semitism. Men could understand political persecution, particularly of Communists who, after all, had been sent to prison merely for the crime of being Communists even in England. Men could understand nationalistic ranting, which happened in every country. But they were outraged by the racial campaign against the Jews. It was no use pleading that nearly every country had had its anti-Semitic episodes or that anti-Semitism was as old as European civilization. Twentieth-century Europe was expected to have outgrown it and, indeed, avowed anti-Semitism now flourished only in the more backward areas. Until the coming of Hitler, Jews enjoyed better conditions in Germany than in almost any other European country, and this made the reversion to barbarism the more flagrant. It was also more barbarous. Anti-Semitism elsewhere was social – the exclusion of Jews from clubs or professions; at worst, a legal limitation in universities. Nazi anti-Semitism was, from the first, brutal and physical. It sickened every civilized conscience. The revolt of conscience, however, did not go far. British public opinion, for instance, voiced its abhorrence of Nazi anti-Semitism and then acquiesced in the restrictions which hampered Jews from finding a refuge in Great Britain. Still, dislike of Hitler's virulent form of anti-Semitism was the decisive force which turned democratic opinion against him. It even overshadowed the anti-Communism which had been his greatest asset abroad as well as at home.

Anti-Fascism was a negative affair, as its name implied. There was in it always an implication of 'resistance' – a confession that Fascism was winning and should be stopped. There was very little idea of doing things more successfully in a democratic way. President Franklin D. Roosevelt did this in the United States, but he had no European imitators. Civilization was supposed to be on the defensive. It had to be maintained, protected, preserved. Pétain's cry at Verdun was resurrected: 'They shall not pass.' Defensive battles are uninspiring, and anti-Fascism was uninspiring except in denunciation. Battles were fought with courage and determination, usually also with despair. They were battles, too, on the fringe of Fascism, remote from Hitler or even benefiting him. The first such battle was

128 Vienna flats before bombardment in 1934. The Karl-Marx-Hof

the Austrian civil war of February 1934 between the Social Democrats and the clericals. Both had much reason to oppose and to fear Hitler; both wanted an independent Austria; but old quarrels drove them apart. The clericals disliked the Social Democrats and therefore imagined that they themselves must be Fascists. They even imagined that, by suppressing the Social Democrats, they would win Mussolini's protection against Hitler. The Austrian Social Democrats were tougher than the German and resisted. There was armed conflict. The blocks of working-class flats, which had been admired throughout Europe, were bombarded by the government forces – a curious gesture of clericalist civilization. Austrian democracy ended. A pallid Fascism took its place, already helpless before Hitler's nationalist gaze.

The Spanish civil war was a graver affair, though also less relevant to the conflict against Fascism than was thought at the time. Spain had been a more or less democratic country since 1931. In 1936 the associated parties of the Left – Radical, Socialist, and Communist – won a general election, though only just. Disgruntled generals staged a military revolt, which the government answered by arming the

factory workers, and their untrained militia successfully resisted the professional forces. What had been intended as a quick *coup d'état* turned into a prolonged civil war. Fascist Italy and Nazi Germany aided the rebels; Soviet Russia aided the government, though on a smaller scale, and anti-Fascists from many other countries also rallied to the government's side. The Spanish civil war provided the fascinating case of a nineteenth-century struggle, fought with twentieth-century phrases and twentieth-century equipment. The rebels stood

129 *Guernika*, Picasso's vision of the Spanish Civil War

for Black Reaction in the conventional sense – clericalism, obscurantism, military dictatorship. Metternich would have felt at home among them. The most stalwart fighters for the government were Anarchists, an equally old-fashioned cause. The International Brigade itself was a reappearance of Garibaldi's Red Shirts, with much the same virtues and much the same faults. Men translated this into the contemporary terms of a struggle between Fascism and democracy, or between Fascism and Communism.

147

The struggle washed over into the world of art and literature. Poets from many countries followed the example of Byron in their poetry and sometimes in their lives. André Malraux, a great French novelist, fought in Spain. Ernest Hemingway, the American, wrote a popular novel about the civil war. Vaughan Williams, the veteran English composer, abandoned folk-music for a new harsh style of symphonies, which voiced the struggle against Fascism. When German aeroplanes obliterated the Basque village of Guernica, Picasso, the greatest painter of the day, expressed his abhorrence in one of his most famous pictures. Casals, the 'cellist, gave concerts on behalf of the republic and, though a Spaniard, refused to return to his native land after the victory of Fascism. Perhaps there has never been a greater mobilization of culture for an ideological cause.

The demonstration was confined to a minority, though by no means all of the intellectual class. While anti-Fascism dominated the men of words and arts, most people were absorbed in a civilized life of a more practical kind. The 1930s, despite the Great Depression, saw also the beginnings of universal prosperity – for all, not for a few. Europe at last reaped the dividends from a century of investment in modern industry. There were motor-cars by the million. More people took holidays away from home, many of them holidays with pay. By 1939, nearly half the people of Europe were reading a newspaper every day. The greatest cultural advance was the 'talkie' – words at last married to pictures on the cinema screen. There was no one dominant figure, as Chaplin had dominated the silent film. Greta Garbo came nearest to it – a sex symbol who now appears in retrospect astonishingly sexless. American Hollywood still had the most money and produced the most films. On the other hand, there was now a language barrier, as there had not been in the silent days. Germany before the Nazis and France throughout the decade produced films of individual quality. English people spoke the same language as Americans, or at any rate could understand more or less the language of American films. This may well have increased the traditional English feeling that they were not really Europeans and that Great Britain had a special relationship with the United States.

130 Film goddess. Greta Garbo in mid-career

131 *The Miracle*. Max Reinhardt rehearsing with Lady Diana Manners in preparation for their great international success

It is doubtful whether more than a conservative minority of Americans reciprocated this feeling.

The British detachment from Europe was more genuine. On the simplest level, all Europe looked alike – the same sort of peasant houses, the same town streets, even the same trams everywhere. England looked different – the houses were lower and differently arranged, the trams and buses were two-deckers. The English Channel was the greatest dividing line in Europe, culturally even deeper than the line between Communism and capitalism. Most English people had ceased to think that their political system was suitable for export. The secrets of constitutional propriety were theirs alone, and perhaps nothing surprised Continental Europeans more than the ease with which the British unloaded themselves of a king, Edward VIII, in 1936. The detachment worked also in political affairs. While most European countries had a sizeable Fascist Party or at least a Fascist threat, the British silenced Sir Oswald Mosley and his Black-shirts with the most trivial effort. Similarly, Hitler was regarded as a nuisance or danger to others, not to the British themselves. Even when Hitler struck the first decisive blow against the settlement of 1919 by reoccupying the Rhineland in 1936, the British government and, for that matter, the British people were only concerned that the French should acquiesce without fuss, as indeed they did.

132 Fallen King.
Edward VIII
announcing
his abdication

European civilization put on its last show at the World Exhibition which was held in Paris in 1937, strange successor to the Great Exhibition which the Prince Consort had organized at Hyde Park in 1851. There was a similar display of mechanical achievements, this time principally of aeroplanes and motor-cars. The French added their peculiar contribution to civilization by a row of booths, at which French alcoholic drinks, including medicinal wines, were distributed free. But whereas the Great Exhibition had preached Free Trade and universal peace, the Exhibition of 1937 displayed the rivalries of creeds and nations. The Soviet pavilion was crowned by a large statue of a half-naked pair, proclaiming the glories of Communism. Directly facing this, the German pavilion was crowned by an equally large eagle, proclaiming the glories of National Socialism. The principal feature of the British pavilion was a blown-up photograph of Neville Chamberlain, the Prime Minister, fishing. Many of the pavilions were never completed, thanks to the strikes which then dominated French economic life. Every country used large graphs to show its achievements. By this device Portugal appeared to outdo all others in the campaign against illiteracy. If you start with one literate man, the graph goes sharply upwards if you end with 100. European civilization was symbolized by graphs which ended with a question mark.

The greatest question mark was against Germany's place in Europe. Early in 1938 the territorial order of Versailles began to crumble when Austria fell unresistingly under Hitler's control. The British and French governments were fairly confident that they could maintain the security of their own countries, except from air attack. They did not believe that they could effectively retard the advance of Germany in eastern Europe. Nor were the British, at any rate, eager to do so. They still supposed that increased prosperity was the cure for Nazi barbarism and therefore looked without regret on an expansion of Germany's economic sphere in regions remote from their own. Moreover, British statesmen proposed that Europe should settle its own affairs without bringing in the two world powers, Soviet Russia and the United States. This was partly a recognition of reality: neither of the world powers was willing to be involved.

133 Rival pavilions. At the Paris Exhibition of 1937 the USSR (right) and Nazi Germany (left) faced each other

Also, Soviet Russia seemed to be a poor associate at the height of the great purge, when Stalin, for some reason still unknown, 'liquidated' almost every prominent Soviet citizen. But there was also an element of European pride, a determination not to confess that Europe's day of mastery was over. 'Hands off Europe' was the cry with which the European ship went down.

Neville Chamberlain, the British Prime Minister, believed that he could handle Hitler. Somewhere in this extraordinary creature must lurk a reasonable man, and this reasonable man would come to the surface once he was convinced that he could get his way by negotiation, not by war. Chamberlain was determined to convince him. His object was to get ahead of Hitler and to give him what he wanted before he asked for it. Czechoslovakia, with its three million German-speaking citizens, was next on the list and, while the ultimate impulse came from fear of German ambitions, British policy gave to the Czech crisis its pattern and timing. The Czechs were pushed into making concessions to their Germans. When these failed to satisfy, Chamberlain took the initiative in proposing that Czechoslovakia should be dismembered. The French tailed reluctantly along. There were alarms of war. At the last moment, or so it seemed, the great men of Europe met at Munich: Hitler, Mussolini, Chamberlain, and Daladier of France together in one room for the first and last time. Neither Stalin nor President Roosevelt was invited. Czechoslovakia was successfully dismembered. Chamberlain proclaimed: 'It is peace for our time.' The conference of Munich took its proud place along with the Congress of Vienna and the peace conference of Paris.

Greater Germany had come at last; the Radical dreams of 1848 were belatedly fulfilled. No doubt Germany would make further gains. Lord Halifax, the British Foreign Secretary, cheerfully opined that Poland and other countries of eastern Europe could presumably only fall more and more into the German orbit. But it was also assumed that Germany would now move in a more leisurely way and that her internal conditions would become less brutal. Neither of these things happened. In November 1938 there was a new and more savage outbreak of anti-Semitism in Germany, stirring dormant consciences again. This was perhaps the moment when most men of goodwill despaired that Germany would ever return to decent human behaviour so long as Hitler ruled. There was still no clear idea what moral should be drawn from this, but at least fewer people believed that concession would do any good. Moreover, Hitler now ran against the one state, Poland, which was determined to make no concessions. Independent Poland, as restored in 1919,

134 Blessed are the peacemakers. Chamberlain, Daladier, Hitler, Mussolini and Ciano at the Munich conference in October 1938

had been a product of that strange, temporary situation, when neither Germany nor Russia counted as Great Powers. Though this situation was now ended, the rulers of Poland believed that their only chance was to behave as proudly as before. Others had trembled and cringed before Hitler; they defied him.

In March 1939 the hopes of Munich were dispelled. Czechoslovakia fell apart. Hitler occupied Prague, with his usual accompaniment of anti-Semitism and the Gestapo. In England the opponents of appeasement seemed vindicated. Chamberlain was swept along by the current. He spoke, somewhat bleatingly, words of resistance: Hitler must somehow be deterred. The means were soon at hand. Poland was allegedly exposed to German threats, and on 31 March the British government guaranteed Poland against aggression. From this moment both Great Britain and France were on the hook.

Neither of them could do anything effective to aid Poland if she were attacked. Equally, there was no way in which they could wring concessions or surrender from the Poles, short of abdicating as Great Powers. They could only hope that nothing would happen; yet they knew that something would. Hitler was still confident that he would establish a Nazi New Order throughout Europe. The other European statesmen – Mussolini as much as Chamberlain and Daladier – went through the motions of living after the fashion of a man in the condemned cell who still enjoys his meals. Old habits of statecraft were pursued, for want of anything better – gestures of defiance, gestures of appeasement, all meaningless like a hen running round the farmyard ten minutes after its head has been cut off.

The British and French governments put on an act of seeking an alliance with Soviet Russia, alliance which they neither wanted nor expected to get. The British government also dangled before Hitler's unimpressed eyes the prospect of a £1,000 million loan if only he would disarm. Hitler was merely encouraged to believe that the

135, 136 War again
German and British
styles of proclamatio

remaining obstacles against him would crumble if he leant harder. He therefore leant. The German army ostentatiously prepared for war against Poland. The Soviet government, who were perhaps never eager for alliance with the western powers, despaired in any case of attaining it and on 23 August signed a neutrality pact with Germany. Hitler probably expected that this would cause his opponents to collapse. Great Britain and France would join him in forcing surrender on the Poles, as they had done with the Czechs – perhaps after a short German war against Poland, perhaps without. The French government were not altogether averse from this course, but Chamberlain was taken prisoner by British public opinion. The British people were determined to stand by the Poles, though they did not know how. Honour, anti-Fascism, the pride of a Great Power, outraged human decency, were mixed together.

Behind the scenes Chamberlain still aspired to a new Munich. He fed Hitler with promises of appeasement and tried to extract concessions from the Poles. Chamberlain and Halifax moved too slowly;

Hitler moved too fast. On 1 September, German armies invaded Poland. Mussolini proposed a conference. The British and French governments held out their tongues in anticipation. The British House of Commons revolted. On 3 September, Chamberlain was constrained to declare war against Germany, to his surprise and bewilderment. The French government followed suit, even more bewildered. Mussolini announced his non-belligerence. Soviet Russia and the United States remained neutral. The Second World War started as a private European venture, European civilization's latest gift to the world.

137 Out of date.
Käthe Kollwitz's
pacifist poster of 1924
says 'No more war'

The Second World War was the most devastating experience, both physically and morally, of European man. Twenty-five million people were killed, cities were obliterated. The Germans committed horrors which have few parallels in recorded history and none in the history of Europe. Moreover, during the war and after it, Europe lost her remaining hegemony over other parts of the world. It is not surprising that men talked of decline or even announced Europe's end. Paradoxically, recovery was also faster and more complete than after any previous catastrophe. Twenty years after the end of the war, the peoples of Europe were more prosperous, more pacific towards each other and, on the whole, more humane in their behaviour than they had ever been. Certainly, the United States outstripped Europe in wealth and economic power. Otherwise, the gap between Europe's standard of life and that outside Europe was wider than it had been at the height of her hegemony and grew still wider each year. Civilization had its gains as well as its drawbacks. The very forces which almost destroyed Europe also restored her. Still, the Second World War shook European civilization and was unpleasant in the extreme while it lasted.

The transition from peace to war was less startling in 1939 than it had been in 1914. This time men's minds were prepared for war, though not necessarily for the war which actually happened. The institutions of war did not have to be improvised while the war was going on; they were all prepared, according to precedents. Many were already operating: the German state, for instance, was already on a war basis. Hitler had almost complete dictatorial powers. The Press was rigidly controlled. Economic life was directed by the state, even though most of it remained theoretically in private hands. Virtually no changes were made when war actually broke out. Thus, paradoxically, Germany, which had been the most warlike of states in peacetime, remained the most peacelike state in war and, in the words of Burton Klein, continued to operate 'a peacelike war economy' until 1943.

Even the democratic states were well on the way to war before-hand. Great Britain had begun to produce armaments without considering financial limitations in February 1939 and had gone over to compulsory military service in March. Now nothing further was done. Armaments were not produced any faster until May 1940. The military call-up proceeded on its leisurely way, with the intention of producing an army of some size only by 1942. The French government had long been operating by decree-laws and simply continued to do so. The only novelty was to declare the Communist Party illegal, a precaution which seemed unnecessary in Great Britain. Other measures of war-regulation, such as rationing, direction of labour and, even in Great Britain, the indignity of identity cards, were introduced without fuss, almost without being noticed. No fuss, no excitement were indeed the features of the Second World War in its early stages. Chamberlain and Daladier, who had been uninspiring leaders in peacetime, remained uninspiring leaders in wartime. There were no new demagogues on the Horatio Bottomley pattern, no cheering crowds or patriotic demonstrations. The war became a routine affair, conducted without enthusiasm by competent civil servants.

The second war also took longer than the first to become a general engagement. In 1914 every European Great Power except Italy was in the war from the beginning, and all except Russia remained in it to the end. The second war began as a limited conflict between Germany on the one side and France, Great Britain, and Poland on the other. It spread more widely in April and May 1940, when Germany overran Norway, Denmark, and the Low Countries, and in June 1940, when Italy entered the war on the German side. There was a further expansion in April 1941, when Germany invaded the Balkans, and a much greater expansion when she attacked Russia in June. The war became world-wide in December 1941, when Japan attacked Pearl Harbor, and Germany and Italy declared war against the United States. Great Britain, her Dominions and, theoretically,

138 Easy victory, German soldiers, after their successful *Blitzkrieg*, parade through Warsaw in October, 1939

Poland were the only countries which went through the Second World War from beginning to end, and it is not possible to fix a precise date when this second war really deserved its name. Few people can now remember the exact day when it ended.

The war refused to start even when it had been declared. The Germans conquered Poland within a month. Soviet forces occupied the eastern lands of Poland as had been arranged in the Nazi-Soviet pact, ostensibly an act of liberation and of protection against the Germans. The British and French did precisely nothing to fulfil the promises which they had given to the Poles. There was nothing they could do, or so their rulers supposed. The Allies intended to win the war without fighting. Stuffed with legends about the weakness of the German economic system (which they were now doing their best to imitate), they believed that Germany would fall down of herself after a year or two. Meanwhile the British and French would build up their armed forces and, when Germany collapsed, these would march in to save her from Bolshevism. The Allies believed, quite wrongly, that blockade had won the first war and so imposed a fresh blockade, which, with Italy and Soviet Russia neutral, caused more trouble to the Allies than to Germany. The Allies also supposed that they had almost limitless financial resources and would thus be able to draw without stint, or without obligation, on the economic strength of the United States. American industry would somehow win the war for the Allies, who would remain free to conduct their own policy – if they had one.

Policy was not much talked about; in a sense, it dictated itself. The Allies this time did not wish to carry off new chunks of the world: they had more than enough already. They were fighting a purely defensive war, and security was their only aim. They could achieve this only by getting rid of Hitler. They had not wanted to go to war against him, but, once in, there was no way out except Hitler's over-throw. And however much this was put in personal terms, it meant the destruction of the Nazi system and the Nazi state. The Germans were not likely to agree to this except after total defeat. Hence the Allies were stuck from the start with the policy of unconditional surrender. The British and French leaders, apart from Churchill, did not welcome this. Their professions of faith in democracy rang faint and thin. Association with the real anti-Fascist forces, at home or abroad, was the last thing they contemplated. But there was no escape for them. They were condemned to become crusaders in a total war.

The 'phoney war', as it was called, also dictated Hitler's future policy. The Germans now ruled Poland, except for the territories which Soviet Russia had carried off. They had achieved the begin-nings of 'living space': what were they to do with it? Poland was exploited for the benefit of German industry. Germans were settled on Polish land. Moreover, the driving force in Hitler's doctrine was racialism. The Poles were an inferior race and must be pushed back into the inferiority from which they ought never to have escaped. Their standard of life was deliberately cut down. They were deprived of education, in the belief that an illiterate people ceased to exist as a nation. These brutal measures were logical conclusions from what had been, in the nineteenth century, respectable academic doctrines. Almost every historian and sociologist then talked about superior and inferior races. Add to this the idea of directing events instead of letting them happen – an idea held by many Socialists and applied in the Soviet five-year plan; transfer it from economics to racialism; and Hitler's New Order was the result. Whereas previously nations had gone up and down in power and cultural prestige according to what happened to them, Hitler was now artificially pushing the Germans up the ladder and everyone else down. Of course, Germany had also to be made stronger for war. But the New Order was more than this; as with most other things which Hitler did, it was the literal application of claptrap which professors had talked in their lecture-rooms.

There was more to come. If the Poles were really inferior, if they were encumbering living space which was needed by the Germans, why stop at reducing their physical and intellectual standards? Why not exterminate them, as the Americans had tried to do with the Red Indians? The war itself pushed Hitler's logic on. The superior races were killing each other, or preparing to do so. The balance should be kept even by killing off the inferior races as well. From start to finish, Hitler was a distorting mirror held up to European civilization, and, when we consider some parts of the European record, not all that distorted. In the first months of the war, the policy of extermination was not yet worked out or fully applied; but its principles had been established and, as Hitler's power over Europe increased, his eagerness to alter the European balance of populations increased also, particularly to the detriment of the Jews. It is said that many Germans regretted this policy of Hitler's. There is little record that they did anything against it. His few opponents, or rather secret critics, were merely afraid that he might after all lose the war.

Here, too, Hitler was pushed by the situation into paths along which he was not sorry to go. Ostensibly he had nothing more to fight for once Poland was conquered, and he made a public offer of peace in October 1939. The Allies did not respond. Hitler was now in the position which Napoleon reached: no one believed that he

would keep his word. There was no chance for him to settle down as a respectable ruler, even if he had wanted to do so. He had to make further conquests. It is said that Germany's economic position made quick success necessary; but action was mainly imposed upon Hitler by the situation. The Allies relied on time. Hitler aimed to deprive them of it. Besides, his temperament grew more adventurous with success; each quick victory tempted him towards the next.

Hitler's first aggression in 1940 was ostensibly defensive in purpose: to secure his Scandinavian flank against an Allied encroachment which he correctly anticipated. His next thrust was to invade Holland and Belgium. Gamelin, the Supreme Commander on the Allied side, imagined that he was faced with a repetition of the Schlieffen plan, and the British and French armies advanced into Belgium to meet the invader. The Germans had, in fact, a new plan: they broke through the French line farther south and swept, almost unimpeded, to the Channel, cutting off the British and French forces in Belgium

139 The first setback.
Allied soldiers
waiting on the beach
at Dunkirk
to be ferried back
to England

from their supplies. Most of the British and some of the French were evacuated from Dunkirk, though with the loss of all their heavy equipment. The French army lost nearly half its strength, and was then shattered by a renewed German attack. Six weeks after fighting started on the western front, France concluded an armistice of almost complete surrender. The verdict of the First World War had indeed been reversed.

German prestige soared; the German officer corps seemed to have vindicated their unique skill. This admiration was not altogether deserved. It is true that some German generals had learnt from Liddell Hart how to use tanks effectively, when others, particularly British generals, regarded him as a nuisance and a crank. But the strategical breakthrough at Sedan, which was the original cause of Germany's victory, had derived mainly from Hitler's inspiration, and from this moment no German general dared challenge his direction of the war.

140 He understood modern war.
Liddell Hart,
who contributed to
major advances
in military techniques

The defeat of France was more than a military event. It marked the apparent end of France as a Great Power and the apparent defeat also of the principles which France had represented. The French armies were no doubt badly directed, but most contemporary observers also thought, whether rightly or wrongly, that the French nation had lost the will to greatness. Memories of the First World War hung heavy over the land. The propertied class could not think why they had ever become involved in war against Hitler. Many of them preferred him to their own Socialists. The ordinary Frenchmen had no faith in their leaders. The war had been tolerable to the French people only so long as no one got hurt. Once fighting had started, they had little thought except that it should be ended. The French had no driving force, no inner conviction, which sustained them. They had come to believe that civilization meant a more comfortable life and particularly two good meals a day. War threatened these comforts, and the French surrendered in order to preserve what they regarded as civilization. Maybe the French lost their bearings because of the rapidity of their military defeat. Others, who held out more resolutely, had a longer breathing-space in which to steel their nerves. At any rate, most Frenchmen supported their new ruler, Marshal Pétain, when he accepted defeat and repudiated the democratic republic.

Germany was supreme in Europe from the Bay of Biscay to the frontiers of Soviet Russia. A few states remained nominally independent and two, Sweden and Switzerland, kept some genuine neutrality. Italy entered the war in June 1940 from a mistaken belief that it was over, and Mussolini was able to appear as Hitler's equal. Otherwise, the twelve months from the fall of France to Germany's attack on Russia were the year of the Nazi German Empire. There was at first little resistance to the Germans in the territories they had conquered; on the contrary, there was in every country a considerable body of collaborators – some merely on the make, some of Fascist conviction, predominantly men, impatient with national divisions, who wanted a united Europe and hoped that Hitler would give it to them. The Germans had long asserted that they were an imperial people and had complained against the historical lot which failed to provide them with an empire. Europe was now more united than it had been even in the time of Napoleon, and under German direction. The Germans had the chance to show what they could do.

141 The man who did
not understand.
Marshal Pétain

142, 143 Monuments of German civilization. The message on the main gate of Auschwitz concentration camp: 'Work Means Freedom'. Far right, Belsen, 1945

The New Order, as Hitler called it, was a test for German leadership, a test also for any project of European unity. It was not a test which either passed with credit. The Germans ran Europe solely for their own benefit. This was partly to nourish their war machine, but it was much more to provide the Germans with the higher standard of life to which, as the superior or master race, they were entitled. Of course, most empires had been run like this, but they are believed to have possessed some moral purpose or, at least, to have been regarded with some respect by the peoples whom they conquered and exploited. The Germans had no claim to moral superiority except that they were Germans, and most of the conquered peoples were unmoved by this claim. Besides, Europeans had been growing more considerate and tolerant; exploitation now needed some excuse and some disguise. The German exploitation had none. It was simply a planned attempt to ensure that the Germans should be better off than anyone else. The plans were organized with much ingenuity, and enforced with great brutality when they encountered resistance. But they represented no general European interest. Indeed they revived national consciousness everywhere, more than years of independence had done.

The dislike for this German empire was heightened when the Germans insisted on bringing with them their anti-Semitic outlook and policy. The extension of this policy across Europe necessarily made it more ruthless and more extreme. It had been possible to imagine, before the war, that the Jews in Germany, a comparatively small number, could be 'eliminated' by expulsion or even voluntary emigration. Now the Germans had some millions of Jews in their power, and they could not simply be turned out. They could only be exterminated. This policy was now adopted with every refinement of civilized skill. The Jews were segregated in nearly every European country. The able-bodied were worked to death. Women and children and the elderly were at first massacred. When this method proved too slow, they were consigned to gas-chambers of a most scientific type. Every civilization has its characteristic monuments: Rome had the gladiatorial arenas, the Middle Ages had cathedrals, the nineteenth century had factories and railway-stations. The monument of German civilization was the death camp of Auschwitz. It was pleaded later that these mass murders were the aberration of a few Nazis or even solely of Hitler himself. In fact, they were an intrinsic part of the New Order, operated sometimes, perhaps, from blind loyalty, and more often from conviction. Few attempts were made to retard its working. The Roman Catholic Church, itself menaced by Hitler, made no official protest, though individual Christians did so, especially outside Germany.

This inexcusable work was also excused later as a by-product of war's destructiveness. The war continued, against the expectation of many. The British Isles remained inviolate, and the British people were resolute for war. Posterity may marvel at this obstinacy. The British, who had been told so often that they were Europeans, now displayed their secret confidence that they were not part of Europe after all. This confidence was justified by geography. The Channel proved an effective barrier against German tanks; if it had not existed, Great Britain would have been overrun even more easily than France. The Channel proved also to be a barrier against ideas. The European obsession with Fascism hardly reached England, despite occasional alarms. Even the most reactionary Englishman did not really think, as many rich Frenchmen did, that Hitler's rule was preferable to that of native Socialists. On the other side, few industrial workers thought that this was a bosses' war which did not concern them. National unity was almost complete. It was symbolized by the partnership between Winston Churchill, aristocratic Tory, and Ernest Bevin, secretary of Great Britain's largest trade union.

The main British motive for continuing the war was plain old-fashioned patriotism – a mixture of pride and ignorance which had almost died out on the Continent. The British Empire had been for centuries a Great Power. Few British people appreciated its present weakness. Even those who did so believed that defeat and destruction were better than surrender. The British dislike of Hitler and the Nazis had very little high principle or idealism about it, despite the anti-Fascist phrases of the time. British people had been deceived, or so they thought, by the stories about German atrocities during the First World War. They therefore refused to believe, or at any rate disregarded, similar stories now, though the stories were in fact rather less than the truth. Hitler was simply regarded as a nuisance who had to be destroyed like a buzzing fly. There was also an assumption that, once this had been done, peace and democracy would again flourish

144 Associates
of wartime,
Churchill
and Ernest Bevin

of themselves. The British war aims therefore, though grandiose, were also essentially negative: to reverse what Hitler had done, to restore what had existed before. Every conquered country was to be liberated; National Socialism was to be destroyed. Many people, some of them British, imagined that Great Britain after the war would lead a free, perhaps a Socialist, Europe. This was never in the spirit of British policy. Once Europeans were freed, they were to be left to their own devices. Indeed, in aiming to destroy National Socialism, the British were also implicitly concerned to destroy European unity as well.

These high speculations were remote in the summer of 1940. The British were then fully occupied with the struggle to survive. Hitler had not contemplated a direct attack on Great Britain. If he considered the matter at all, he assumed, as most Continentals did, that she would make peace once she lost her European allies. His plans for invasion had to be hastily improvised, without either landing-craft or an air force designed for the purpose. The British were saved in part by the Royal Navy, on which they had always relied, and more by the fighter aeroplanes, on which until recently even the experts had not relied at all. The dogma that bombers would always get through was nowhere held more strongly than in Great Britain. It was in British skies that the dogma was now disproved. The German air force was defeated, though by a smaller margin than the British believed at the time. Hitler was not gravely perturbed by this failure, for he was convinced, almost with justification, that submarine blockade would gradually reduce Great Britain to collapse and surrender. He was also convinced, with somewhat more justification, that the British could do him little harm even while they continued the war. Germany reverted almost to peacetime conditions: much of the army was demobilized, industry reduced its production of munitions. The war, it seemed, was over, though the British refused to acknowledge it.

The British were faced with a long struggle merely to remain independent. They undertook it with equanimity and efficiency. No country has ever been organized for war so completely and with such general agreement. War Socialism was a common phrase in both wars: Great Britain provided the most perfect and successful example of it. All industrial life was controlled and planned for war purposes. There was direction of labour. Women were conscripted both for the services and into industry. Rationing extended from food to clothes and furniture, ultimately to almost everything. Over two million people were evacuated from the large towns and distributed over the countryside. Yet, at this time of national emergency, welfare services for the poor and the dependent enormously increased. This was an egalitarian society, perhaps the most complete there has ever been. Much of it was done by voluntary arrangement; all of it with hardly a murmur of complaint. In the first alarm of 1940 the British interned all enemy aliens. Soon afterwards they released nearly all and often welcomed them into the armed forces. Even the handful of eccentrics who had openly displayed sympathy with Hitler were later released. Here was Socialism without compulsion; Socialism without a secret police or labour camps. Perhaps it showed that the British were a very odd people who managed to combine liberty and total war. The entire set-up was dismantled after the war.

It left no mark on contemporary civilization, and not much even on the British people. But it enabled them to survive.

The British might have been expected to be content, even delighted, that they survived with the entire Continent organized against them. At most, their historic role was to keep the war going until Hitler somehow brought new enemies down upon himself. The British wanted to do more: they wanted to defeat Hitler all by themselves, and many of them, including some in high places, supposed that they could do it. The stale legends about German economic weakness still persisted, despite the manifest facts to the contrary. The extent and the power of European resistance to the Germans were greatly exaggerated. The resources of the British Empire were exaggerated also. The British believed, with more reason, that they would be able to draw on the almost limitless strength of the United States, but did not appreciate that this strength would take time to mobilize nor that American aid would be given only on stern conditions. The greatest British reliance, however, was on air-power, a weapon with which they hoped actually to win the war. This confidence, though misplaced, largely shaped the character of European civilization during the Second World War.

The overwhelming and irresistible nature of bombardment from the air had been a widely held doctrine ever since the First World War. Statesmen had acknowledged it and novelists had written books about it. The Spanish civil war had been wrongly supposed to confirm it. No country, except one, had prepared to apply the doctrine in practice. Nearly every air force, including particularly the German, was designed to act in close co-operation with the ground forces. Only the British had a force intended for independent, or, as it was called, strategical bombing. The Royal Air Force was not, in fact, equipped for this purpose. It had been assumed that bombers would be able to fly unresisted over enemy territory in daylight – the only condition on which accurate bombing was then possible. Experience soon showed that these bombers would be destroyed by faster, short-range enemy fighters, and daylight bombing eventually had to be abandoned. But the British were determined to drop bombs somehow. With virtually no army, with no foothold on

the Continent, and with no European allies, it seemed the only way in which they could strike against Germany. They therefore launched a campaign of night raids, which was continued intermittently throughout the war.

The campaign was started with aeroplanes inadequate both in number and equipment. Then British industry was devoted to the mass-production of bombers; great scientific ingenuity went into improving them. The German measures of defence also improved. Though great destruction was caused to German cities, the sending of bombers over Germany imposed a strain on the British economy which was greater than its damage to the German. The Germans had a similar experience. They sought to retaliate in kind and improvised

145, 146, 147 Second World War art. *The Siege of Monte Cassino,* by a German painter (opposite); bomb damage to Somerset House in Bath, by John Piper, one of the official war artists (above); an underground shelter as seen by Henry Moore (below)

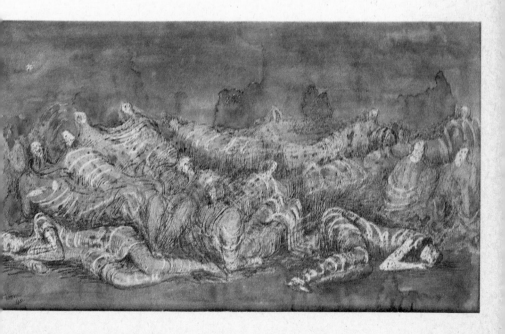

148, 149 After the raids. Coventry severely damaged in 1940 (left), and a street scene in Hamburg in 1943

a series of night attacks, known as the Blitz, with aeroplanes hastily adapted for the purpose. The German raids, too, did not seriously affect British production, though they gave British people an unpleasant winter. Independent bombing achieved no decisive results until 1944, when the Americans produced a long-range fighter which enabled daylight raids to be resumed.

Night bombing, though ineffective as a means of war, had profound moral consequences. It completed the psychology of total war. At first, it claimed to be strictly strategical and to aim only at munitions factories and military installations. When it proved impossible to hit these targets, the objective was changed to the houses of workers in war production, and this, in its turn, soon merged into indiscriminate destruction, directed against the civilian population.

177

The Germans were to be battered down, and made eager to surrender. Even this calculation did not work. In Germany, as previously in Great Britain, indiscriminate bombing increased the people's will to war, and German war production reached its height in 1944, exactly at the moment when British bombing also reached its height. What mattered was the outlook: the readiness, by the British, of all people, to stop at nothing when waging war. Civilized restraints, all considerations of morality, were abandoned. By the end of the war, men were not only ready to kill countless women and children; they also cheerfully used a weapon which endangered future generations. This was the legacy of the bombing strategy which the British adopted with such high-minded motives.

Bombing was not the only British legacy in the Second World War. There was another, more strictly strategical: the decision to turn such military strength as the British possessed against Italy. The decision sprang from the simple practical motive that, while the British had no contact with German land forces, they could strike against the Italians in North Africa. The decision was fortified by the argument that the defeat of Italy would deprive Germany of an ally or even give the British a back door into Europe. The practical consequence was that Italy herself later became a theatre of war. Italian cities, which stood among the most precious memorials of European culture, were ravaged by prolonged fighting. When the war ended, the Italian campaign had used up the energies of ten British and Americans for every one German, and the Allied armies were still not on German soil.

It seems clear, in retrospect, that the essential British function was to keep the war going until Hitler somehow brought about his own ruin. This is, at any rate, what happened. Neither Soviet Russia nor the United States was anxious to enter the war. Soviet Russia, on the edge of a hostile continent, put off the evil day by desperate attempts to appease Hitler. The American position was more equivocal. President Roosevelt was eager to help Great Britain and, by means of lend-lease, was able to continue doing so when the British supply of dollars ran out. Great Britain became a poor, though deserving, cousin – not to Roosevelt's regret. So far as it is possible to read his devious mind, it appears that he expected the British to wear down both Germany and themselves. When all independent powers had ceased to exist, the United States would step in and run the world. Despite talk of liberating or even restoring Europe, Roosevelt really assumed that there was no more Europe. The United States would soon engross all the power in the world, with Europe and indeed everywhere else as their grateful dependants.

Hitler's plans for dominating the world were less precise, if indeed he had them. He was preoccupied by his concern to make his domination of Europe secure against all comers. He began to project an invasion of Soviet Russia the moment France was defeated and put the project into operation twelve months later. This invasion was as much the central event of the Second World War as Napoleon's had been of his imperial record. It was the event which made everything happen differently. Hitler gave varying explanations: sometimes he said it was undertaken to deprive Great Britain of a potential ally, sometimes on the assumption that Great Britain had ceased to count. Conquered Russia was to provide both colonial subjects and living space for the German people. At the same time, the Russians were to be liberated and Europe preserved from the barbarities of Communism. In one way or another, the invasion was for Hitler, as for Napoleon, an irresistible temptation: apparently easy, enormously rewarding, and a crusade into the bargain.

Hitler's invasion of Russia ought to have made sense as a culminating point in European civilization. Civilized Europeans, particularly elderly Europeans from the richer classes, had been clamouring for two things ever since the First World War: one was European unity, the other was an attack by civilized, capitalist Europe on Bolshevik Russia. In 1941 Hitler gave civilized Europeans what they had wanted. Yet everything had worked out wrong. The peoples of Europe made little response to Hitler's crusading appeal, apart from a few exceptions, such as General Franco, and his response was not much more than symbolic. On the contrary, most Europeans outside Germany and nearly all who were on the side of freedom actually wanted Soviet Russia to win. This was an extraordinary transformation after twenty-five years of supposedly implacable hostility

150 War in the African desert. German forces on a battlefield between Tobruk and Sidi Omar

between Communism and democracy, even more extraordinary when Soviet Russia was, if anything, less free and more destructive of human lives than Nazi Germany. But so it was: 22 June 1941 was the moment when Russia unwillingly returned to Europe and again became an acknowledged element in European civilization.

The transformation was not undisputed. There were some in England and many more in the United States, including Senator (later President) Truman, who wanted to stand aside while Germans and Russians cut each others' throats. They were silenced by the mighty voice of Winston Churchill, who at once embraced the Soviet cause. Thus Churchill was twice the instrument of destiny: once when he inspired Great Britain to survive as an independent power and again when he brought Soviet Russia into the comity of nations. These were his great achievements, however much he tried to undo the second after the war. President Roosevelt took the same line more cautiously and for more empirical reasons. He took it more readily in December 1941. The United States were pushed into the Second World War a good deal more openly than they had been

151 War in the Russian winter. Soldiers and officers freeing a snow-bound train in 1941

pushed into the First. Indeed, it is difficult to see how the Americans could ever have become involved in the European war on a fighting basis, if Hitler had not gratuitously done it for them.

Roosevelt was less Utopian than Wilson had been. He meant to liberate Europe, in the sense of imposing unconditional surrender on Germany and Italy, the Axis powers. He had less faith in the panacea of a League of Nations. His own device of a United Nations was little more than a cloak for a world directorate, run by the United States and its humble satellite, Great Britain. Every country except the United States and Great Britain was to be disarmed, and the world would then be policed, inspired, and conducted by Roosevelt himself. As time went on, he made certain exceptions to his general plan. One, China, was of no concern to European affairs, particularly as Roosevelt intended that the European powers, including Great Britain, should lose the remnants of their overseas empires. Soviet Russia was a different matter. At first Roosevelt assumed, as many people did, that she would be defeated: there would then be no problem. By the end of 1942 it was clear that she was going to

152, 153 War lords for democracy. Churchill, Stalin and F.D.R.

survive and probably going to win. Roosevelt was not dismayed. He soon became convinced that he could get on better with Stalin than he did with Churchill and was therefore ready to accept Soviet Russia as a partner in running the world. Stalin, he supposed, was an easy-going opportunist much like himself, who asked nothing of the world except that it should keep quiet. This assumption, though maybe wrong about Stalin personally, was not so far astray about Soviet policy as many people imagined when the war ended.

The war had still three and a half years to run – and very long years they seemed to the peoples involved – but, though the war determined the fate of Europe and was increasingly fought on European soil, the peoples of Europe, other than the Germans, contributed comparatively little to it. Germany and Italy were the only Continental powers seriously engaged, and Italy largely fell out when Mussolini was overthrown in July 1943. Great Britain was the only European country fully at war on the anti-German side, and she, as events had shown, was more outside Europe than in. Otherwise, the outcome of this European war depended on Soviet Russia and the United States – the one a power which Europe had done its best to exclude and the other not European at all. Until the last year of the war, the Russians did most of the fighting against Germany. They took on nine-tenths of the German army and wore down German strength. The Americans were diverted by the British into a Mediterranean campaign against Italy, which absorbed most of their forces, and continued this campaign in Italy against the Germans, even when the Italians themselves had been defeated. Otherwise, their main activity, apart from the Far East, was to second the British campaign of indiscriminate bombing. In fact, it looked for some time as though the war would end with the British and Americans in control of the Mediterranean, and Soviet Russia dominant over a largely devastated Continent.

Things did not work out like this. In June 1944 the British and Americans at last landed in northern France and began a victorious campaign which was to carry them to the heart of Germany. This campaign was the high point of scientific, civilized warfare, with an ingenuity and perfection of organization never previously achieved. War caught up with modern times. The war on the eastern front was, of course, conducted with far more weight of metal and machines. The greatest tank battle of all time was fought at Kursk in 1943. Later, the Russians owed part of their success to superior mobility, provided by the hosts of jeeps which they received from the United States. But this eastern war was still a war which turned on manpower: millions of men fought, millions were killed. The Germans added to the slaughter by massacring the civilian populations and prisoners of war.

154 Return to France. Allied troops disembarking on the beach on D-Day, 6 June 1944

In the end, the Russians won because they proved themselves to be harder than the Germans. Their driving force was not an idealistic devotion to Communism, still less fear of the dictatorial state. It was love for their country and hatred of the brutal, invading Germans. In Russia, and nowhere else, the Second World War is called the Great Patriotic War. The old-fashioned emotion of patriotism was stronger in Communist Russia than in any other European country except Great Britain.

Europe was not altogether without a history in the years when others fought over her soil. This history was the Resistance, an episode glorious, even romantic, at the time, which seemingly left little mark. In every conquered country there were some people who did what they could against the Germans. The proportion varied greatly with the will and the opportunity: open countries with good communications, such as France, were easier for the Germans to police than, say, the mountainous districts of Yugoslavia. Some countries were merely conquered by the Germans, and their governments escaped to Great Britain, so that resistance implied no breach with previous loyalties. In some countries the governments collapsed or, as in France, collaborated with the Germans. Here resistance was mixed up with internal conflicts. The first resisters were mainly straightforward patriots, such as General de Gaulle, and their devotion to democracy was often not very evident, as de Gaulle again exemplified. As time went on, there was a tendency for the spirit of the Resistance to swing towards the Left. The simple patriots had either to conform or to be pushed out. Sometimes, as a result, the patriots came very near going over to the German side. A new and powerful element came in when Soviet Russia was invaded. The Communists, who had previously denounced the 'imperialist' war, now became the most determined of resisters and claimed to be the most democratic as well. Though a good deal of this was pretence, the Communists boasted more truly than they knew. After the war they found, to their surprise, that they had become parliamentary parties on the democratic pattern in more than one country.

The Resistance breathed the spirit of the Romantic Age, as though the great days before 1848 had come again. Young Europe was reborn. Whereas in the openly combatant countries everything turned on organization and system, the Resistance was the work of individuals – individual courage, individual enterprise and initiative. Perhaps the contrast helped to shape the different characteristics of occupied and unoccupied countries in the post-war years. The Resistance nowhere actually menaced German rule, except perhaps in parts of Yugoslavia, though it was a serious nuisance and provided valuable aid to the Allied armies when the time came for invasion. What the Resistance did was to keep alive, or to restore, the spirit of national pride. Nearly all the European states had been rolled flat; yet all stood up again after the war more independent than before, thanks largely to the Resistance. The active movement was, of course, everywhere the work of a minority, sometimes of a small minority. For most Europeans, the war ended in 1940, or whenever it was that their country had been conquered. Nevertheless, they could not escape the legacy of the Resistance. It was what they ought to have been doing, and many, no doubt, became resisters after the event.

The legacy of the Resistance varied from country to country. Where it co-operated with an exiled government and that government was then normally restored, it vanished almost unseen into civil life. This happened, for instance, in Holland and Norway, which returned easily to constitutional monarchy. Elsewhere, the Resistance was contending against native authorities as well as against the Germans. France provided the clearest example. General de Gaulle stood almost alone when he raised the standard of resistance in June 1940; most Frenchmen then acknowledged Marshal Pétain and his government at Vichy. Even the few resisters were at first doubtful of de Gaulle – a supposedly democratic leader who had shown no faith in democracy, a general who had virtually never commanded in war. As time passed, de Gaulle took undisputed leadership of the Resistance, a remarkable triumph of personal arrogance. Even the Communists worked under him, though no doubt believing mistakenly that they would later be able to exploit him. De Gaulle and his movement did not contribute greatly to the defeat of the Germans, despite many acts of heroism. The course of the war would not have been markedly different if de Gaulle had not existed.

155, 156 National resistance. De Gaulle was head of the Free French in England; Marshal Tito, at far right, led the Communist partisans to ultimate victory in Yugoslavia

All the same, de Gaulle had a great influence on the future. He reasserted the existence of France, even when she did not exist. He defeated Roosevelt's plans for running liberated Europe under American orders. When the Americans reached Paris in August 1944 they found de Gaulle already installed as head of the French republic. He not only restored France as an independent country, but also as a Great Power. Throughout the war his energies went as much into disputes with Churchill and later with Roosevelt as into combats against the Germans. France, at the end of the war, was devastated, impoverished, and her armed forces were dependent on American supplies; nevertheless, de Gaulle pitched his claims as high as though he were Louis XIV, and he succeeded. France was admitted to the ranks of the Great Powers. The United Nations ceased to be a directorate under American control. Moreover, once France existed again, Europe existed also: de Gaulle led Europe back to independence. Not all his hopes were fulfilled. The French people were not made anew. The true Gaullists were few in number even when de Gaulle, later on, was elected President with almost dictatorial powers. But if Europe now stands in the world as a third force independent both of the United States and Soviet Russia, it is due more to de Gaulle than to any other single man.

In Yugoslavia, Marshal Tito had a similar significance on a smaller scale. The first resistance here came from people far from Communist – army officers and others of a reactionary cast. Their thoughts were on Yugoslavia after the war, and they were reluctant to run risks before the decisive moment of liberation. Tito and his Communists fought immediately in order to demonstrate their existence. They fought without Soviet assistance, perhaps against Soviet wishes. They were able to claim, with some exaggeration, that they had liberated Yugoslavia by independent action, whereas the Communist rulers elsewhere in eastern Europe returned after the war, as Tito said, in Soviet aeroplanes, smoking their pipes.

At the end of the war the western powers lamented that, thanks to Tito, the Soviet Empire had been brought to the shores of the Adriatic. Soon, however, the Yugoslav Communists asserted their independence against Stalin and Soviet Russia. They broke the unity of the international Communist movement and challenged the dictatorship which Stalin had exercised over it. National Communism was the outcome, ultimately even in other countries where Communists ruled. Thus, once again, national independence was displayed as the strongest element in the European legacy.

157, 158 Yugoslav partisans

Resistance also played a part in the two Axis countries, though with widely different effects. There was precious little resistance to Mussolini while he held power, though also, no doubt, little enthusiasm for him. Even his overthrow was a private conspiracy, partly by non-Fascist conservatives, partly by Fascists themselves. Resistance came only when the Allies turned Italy into a battleground. Partisans of many kinds – democrats, belated followers of Garibaldi, Communists – rallied to the cause. The Allies regarded the Resistance with scepticism and even suspicion. It played only a minor part in defeating the Germans, but this part was enough. The sacrifice of lives was great, and the inspiration was beyond dispute. Italy purged herself of twenty years of Fascism and stepped back unchallenged among the democratic peoples. Mussolini left no legacy. He appeared in retrospect only as a bad joke. Italy was truly liberated from Fascism, and she was liberated in spirit by the Italians themselves.

The Germans showed a more equivocal record. There were always Germans who disliked or even opposed Hitler's rule. Communists were active in futile conspiracies, despite the fact that many went over to the Nazi side. The solid Social Democrats contracted out of the Nazi system from start to last. There were also doubters in high places – generals, administrators, members of old aristocratic families. Many of them disliked the savage crimes of Nazi rule, and of course they disliked Hitler himself. Hardly any cared for democracy or regretted the Weimar republic, which some of them, indeed, had helped to overthrow. They were conservatives, traditionalists, often monarchists. What united them was the fear that Hitler was leading Germany to defeat and ruin. They had little objection to his programme of conquest if only he could carry it out, but they did not believe that he could. Here lay their weakness. For a time Hitler succeeded against all the rules. So long as he succeeded, his secret opponents could do nothing against him and perhaps did not want to. Though later dignified with the name of the German Resistance, these men did not in fact resist. They talked of overthrowing Hitler; they made elaborate plans to overthrow him; but they moved against him only in July 1944, when Germany's defeat was already certain, and even then their abortive rising was due to the initiative

159 Red Flag
over Berlin.
Soviet troops
atop the Reichstag,
8 May 1945

of a single man, von Stauffenberg. Their attempt evoked no response. They were leaders without followers, generals without soldiers.

Their failure seemed to show that there was no widespread opposition to Hitler in Germany. At most, it bore witness that not all Germans were unreservedly on Hitler's side. But there was never a popular Resistance in Germany which could inspire a new democratic feeling after the war. Most Germans were at first enthusiastic for Hitler. Later, many were still enthusiastic, and the rest acquiesced. This was not due solely to the extra dash of subservience which some foreign observers attributed to the Germans. The obstacles against Resistance were far greater in Germany than in any other country. Elsewhere, even in Italy after Mussolini's fall, the Resistance stood for national liberation; it was sustained by patriotism. In Germany, resistance, if there had been any, would have involved national defeat and, in a sense, betrayal of the national cause. Hitler's opponents tried to evade this. They sought assurances from the Allies that, if they overthrew Hitler, Germany would be allowed to keep some, at any rate, of his conquests. This was a demand which it was impossible to satisfy. The Allies were committed to 'unconditional surrender' – a full and final liberation which would undo Hitler's achievements, in Germany as well as abroad.

Later on, some men of goodwill lamented that there had not been a sensible and moderate peace of compromise, which would have saved Europe both from destruction and from Communism. They even alleged that unconditional surrender was a compound of Roosevelt's folly and Stalin's wickedness. In fact, compromise was never on offer. Apart from anything else, Hitler barred the way. He was supreme in Germany; his power was never shaken; he knew that he could not survive even moderate defeat and in any case remained confident that he would somehow escape his difficulties as he had always done before. Perhaps new weapons would save him – and they nearly did. If not, the Allies would fall out among them-

160 Hitler's end. The bunker in Berlin where the Führer killed himself

161 Mussolini's end. *Il Duce* and his mistress, Clara Petacci, strung up by Italian partisans in Milan, 29 April 1945

selves. This, too, was not impossibly far-fetched. The old suspicions between the Communist and non-Communist worlds were never far from the surface. We do not know what doubts there were in Soviet counsels, but it is likely that they existed. President Roosevelt, we know, was more confident about the future than many of his associates. When he died in April 1945, his successor, Truman, soon chose anti-Soviet assistants and backed away from co-operation. Churchill claimed later that he had long been sounding the alarm against Stalin – perhaps as early as 1942, certainly by 1944. Unconditional surrender was the only programme which could hold the Allies together, and Hitler remained the guarantor of Allied unity. This was not because total war had released total hatred; it was simply that unconditional surrender was the only sensible way of dealing with Hitler.

This programme was achieved. The Allied armies met on the Elbe. Hitler killed himself. Mussolini was killed by Italian partisans. On 8 May 1945 the German armies surrendered unconditionally.

The German government, which Hitler had posthumously nominated, was ordered out of existence, and the victorious Great Powers set themselves up as the rulers of Germany. There seemed little to prevent their becoming rulers of the world, once Japan had been defeated. The great men met at Potsdam, once the seat of the Hohenzollerns. Truman, Stalin, and Churchill bestrode a recumbent Europe : two world powers, one remote from Europe, the other estranged from it, with Great Britain as a diminished third. The historic continent of Europe had no representative. It was tempting to draw a line and to declare that European civilization had reached its term.

This gloomy view turned out to be mistaken. Potsdam did not prove to be the beginning of a new epoch in the history of the world; rather, it was merely the end of an episode. Between 1939 and 1945 the historic landmarks had been overturned. Germany had dominated the Continent. Two world powers had intervened in Europe against Germany with devastating effect. Once the Germans had surrendered, nearly everything went back, in appearance, to where it had been before. Poland acquired territory in the west from Germany and lost territory in the east to Soviet Russia. Yugoslavia acquired Istria from Italy. Otherwise the frontier posts shot up all over Europe in their old places. No new states appeared; and no old states disappeared, except for the three Baltic states which Soviet Russia had eaten up in 1940.

There was one sharp, brutal transformation. Some seven million Germans vanished in the lands which passed to Poland. Many had been killed; many fled; the rest were driven out. A little later, over three million Germans were expelled from Czechoslovakia in a slightly more orderly manner. This re-sorting of Europeans into their national tribes was a policy which the victors had learnt from Hitler, and not an attractive one. The nationalism which had so long ravaged Europe was carried to its logical culmination. The national states were now more truly national in their composition than they had been before. Otherwise, the Germans paid surprisingly little penalty for their misdeeds. A few German leaders were hanged after a sort of trial – mainly for the crime of having lost. Apart from this, it was soon assumed that, while the atrocious crimes were being committed, all the Germans except Hitler were somewhere else. This version, though unlikely, saved a great deal of trouble and soon became the universally accepted legend.

Where the Soviet armies penetrated, Communist governments were set up, at first in a disguised, later in an open form. The propertied classes were dispossessed. Economic life was directed ostensibly by the state. But the rulers of these supposedly revolutionary countries were middle-class intellectuals, not very different in origin, outlook, and character from the governing classes in the West. A visitor to Warsaw or Budapest, twenty years after the war, remarks that these cities are much more like the cities of western Europe than they are like Moscow. As for western Europe itself, no one can now discover any evidence, apart from an occasional ruin not yet restored, that there was a war at all. The buildings have been rebuilt; nearly everyone is prosperous; democracy is, if anything, stabler and more smooth-running than it used to be. In some countries, Communist parties have become an accepted part of the political system. Even this state of affairs, which seems to be the only serious consequence of the Second World War, was often maturing before then.

162 Partnership dissolved. Stalin, Truman and Churchill meet at Potsdam, July 1945

164 Life goes on. The rebuilding of Dresden, 1966

This remarkable transformation was no doubt assisted by the fact
that the two powers, who dominated the world at the end of the war,
soon fell out. Hitler had frightened them into each other's arms, and
it could hardly be expected that they would remain in close embrace,
once he had disappeared. They proceeded to harbour extravagant
apprehensions against each other. Both again operated from fear – the
Americans from fear of Communism, the Russians from fear of
nuclear weapons. Both sought to enlist European strength, for what
that was worth. In time, it proved a false alarm on both sides. Essentially, the attitude of the two world powers towards Europe was
unchanged: they merely wanted Europe to leave them alone. This
Europe did, now that Germany was out of the running as a Great
Power. Europe had the chance to recover, and Europeans took it.
They were still the most civilized and skilful of all peoples, when war
did not get in the way.

◀ 163 Culture in ruins. The devastation of Dresden after the Allied air-raids of 1945

165 The new Coventry

This was the great paradox in the thirty years between Sarajevo and Potsdam. Europe had two long wars, the most devastating in her history. Europeans flung themselves into these wars with the greatest ingenuity and enthusiasm. No wars have ever been conducted with such solid popular backing. European civilization reached its highest point with the atomic bomb – a European gift to America. Yet Europeans remained almost unaffected by this wild race to destruction. They fought two wars and then did their best to forget about them. The lasting achievements of this European civilization were in peace as much as in war. Tanks were one of its symbols; but so, also, were the motor-cars which filled the roads every week-end. Millions of dead were one symbol. Millions of lives saved, millions of people living healthier lives, were another. More houses were destroyed, and more new houses were built, than in the whole of previous history. Nations asserted their independence, and national differences almost

197

ceased to exist. The capitalist countries planned their economies, and Communist countries preached the virtues of free enterprise.

Europe was supposed to have lost its hegemony in the world. Yet there was no part of the world which did not become European or at any rate did not aspire to do so. Virtually everyone wore European clothes. Virtually every country had some form of European constitution. Virtually every inhabitant of the globe had European ideas and pursued European ambitions. Everyone wanted social services and his own motor-car. Everyone went to the cinema and watched television. Everyone imagined that universal prosperity had arrived or was just round the corner. Civilization had once been the property of a few : now it was claimed by all. Time alone will tell whether the claim can be satisfied. At any rate, it was Europe's legacy to the world, and only civilization of a European pattern can fulfil it.

Land gained by USSR at expense
of Germany, Finland, Poland, Czechoslovakia
and Rumania (Estonia, Latvia and
Lithuania became Soviet Republics)

Extent of Nazi Germany in 1939

REPUBLIC
OF
IRELAND

GREAT BRITAIN

NORWAY

SWEDEN

FINLAND

DENMARK

NETHERLANDS

BELGIUM

WEST GERMANY

EAST
Berlin •
GERMANY

Bonn •

POLAND

UNION OF

SOVIET

SOCIALIST

REPUBLICS

FRANCE

SWITZERLAND

CZECHOSLOVAKIA

AUSTRIA

HUNGARY

RUMANIA

YUGOSLAVIA

BULGARIA

ALBANIA

GREECE

SPAIN

ITALY

166 Europe before and after World War II

BIBLIOGRAPHICAL NOTES

The French produce the most detailed accounts, three works being especially useful. *L'Europe du XIX et XX siècle*, vols. v and vi (1965), covers 1914 until now – the latter being sometimes 1954 and sometimes 1962. Though directed by the Council of Europe, it is stronger on individual countries than on Europe as a whole, and the 'crisis' to which it repeatedly refers was mainly a crisis among intellectuals. *Histoire des relations internationales*, vols. vii and viii (1957–58), by P. Renouvin, covers the years 1914–45 and is much more than a diplomatic history. Even more substantial is vol. vii in the *Histoire générale des civilisations: L'époque contemporaine*, by Maurice Crouzet (1957). This also starts in 1914, but more than half the book is devoted to the world after 1945.

The civil side of the First World War is discussed only in *The War behind the War*, by F.P. Chambers (1939). *Generals and Politicians*, by J.C. King (1951), describes the conflicts behind the scenes in France. *Men and Power*, by Lord Beaverbrook (1956), does the same, more episodically, for Great Britain. German war aims have received much attention, as in *Germany's Drive to the West*, by H.W. Gatzke (1951), and, more recently, in *Griff nach der Weltmacht*, by F. Fischer (1961). *Mitteleuropa in Thought and Action*, by H.C. Meyer (1957), is also important. The rivalry of Lenin and Wilson appears in *Political Origins of the New Diplomacy*, by A.J. Mayer (1959). The Socialist side is developed in *International Labor, Diplomacy and Peace*, by A. van der Slice (1941); see also *The Troublemakers* by the present writer (1957). The breach between Russia and the West is described in *Russia Leaves the War* (1956) and *The Decision to Intervene* (1957), both by G. Kennan. For the end of the war see *Armistice*, by F. Maurice (1943), and *Armistice 1918*, by H. Rudin (1944).

The effects of the First World War are studied in various volumes published by the Carnegie Endowment: *The Consequences of the War* to *Great Britain*, by F. W. Hirst (1934); *The War and German Society*, by A. Mendelssohn-Bartholdy (1937); and *La bilan de la guerre pour la France*, by C. Gide (1931). *The Effect of the War in South-Eastern Europe*, by D. Mitrany (1936), should also be mentioned here.

International history between the wars is summarized in *A Short History of International Affairs*, by G. M. Gathorne-Hardy (1950), and *International Affairs between the Two World Wars*, by E. H. Carr (1940). There is a *History of the League of Nations* by F. P. Walters, 2 vols. (1958). A more general view is given in *The Twenty Years' Crisis*, by E. H. Carr (1946). The most important book on Soviet Russia is *A History of Soviet Russia*, by E. H. Carr, 8 vols. to date (1950–   ). Italian Fascism is described in *Mussolini's Italy*, by H. Finer (1935), and in many inadequate biographies of Mussolini. There is much more on Germany, including a symposium sponsored by UNESCO, *The Third Reich* (1955). *Hitler*, by Alan Bullock (1952), is the best biography. English readers are not allowed to see the full text of *Mein Kampf*, allegedly because it might turn them into Nazis. The Second World War has not yet been digested into scholarly form. The best summary is in *The War: A Concise History, 1939–1945*, by L. L. Snyder (1962).

Escaping from politics to more general themes, there are *Europe on the Move*, by E. M. Kulischer (1948); *Growth and Stagnation in the European Economy*, by I. Svennilson (1954); *The New Outline of Modern Knowledge*, edited by Alan Pryce-Jones (1956); and *An Introduction to Modern Architecture*, by J. M. Richards (1953). The student of civilization will be profitably employed in studying the contemporary literature and works of art. Here is a selection, chronologically arranged: *À la recherche du temps perdu*, by Marcel Proust (1913 et seq.); *Mr Britling Sees it Through*, by H. G. Wells (1916); *Le feu*, by H. Barbusse (1916); *The Decline of the West*, by O. Spengler (1918–22); *The Economic Consequences of the Peace*, by J. M. Keynes (1919); *Six Characters in Search of an Author*, by L. Pirandello (1921); *The Confessions of Zeno*, by I. Svevo (1921); *Wozzeck* (opera), by Alban Berg (1921); *Ulysses*, by James Joyce (1922); *The Waste Land*, by T. S. Eliot (1922); *The Magic Mountain*, by T. Mann (1923); *Les faux monnayeurs*, by A. Gide (1925); *The Trial*, by F. Kafka (1925); *The*

Gold Rush (film), by C. Chaplin; *All Quiet on the Western Front*, by E.M. Remarque (1928); *The Threepenny Opera*, by B. Brecht (1928); *Lady Chatterley's Lover*, by D.H. Lawrence (1928); *La condition humaine*, by A. Malraux (1933); *Fontamara*, by I. Silone (1933); *Language, Truth and Logic*, by A.J. Ayer (1936); *General Theory of Employment*, by J.M. Keynes (1936); *Guernika* (painting), by P. Picasso (1937).

LIST OF ILLUSTRATIONS

1 Painting by George Grosz: *Funeral Procession. Dedicated to Oskar Pannizza*; 1917. Staatsgalerie, Stuttgart

2 Central Station, Milan. Photo: Alinari

3 Paris Opéra. Photo: Thames and Hudson Archive

4 Town Hall, Stockholm. Photo: Svenzk Trafikförbundet

5 Map: Europe before and after World War I. Drawn by Joan Emerson

6 King George V as Emperor of India, Delhi; 1911. Reproduced by Gracious Permission of H.M. the Queen. Royal Library, Windsor

7 Keir Hardie addressing a rally in Trafalgar Square; May 1913. Photo: Radio Times Hulton Picture Library

8 Kaiser Wilhelm greets the King of Italy aboard the yacht *Hohenzollern* in Venice. Photo: Südd. Verlag Bild-Archiv

9 Arrested suffragettes in St James's Park, May 1914. Photo: Radio Times Hulton Picture Library

10 Painting by Georges Braque: *Young Girl with guitar*; 1913. Musée National d'Art Moderne, Paris

11 Painting by Fernand Léger: *City*; 1919. Collection Gallatin, Philadelphia Museum of Art

12 Painting by Oskar Kokoschka: *The Tempest*; 1914. Kunstmuseum, Basel

13 Archduke Ferdinand and his wife entering their car before their assassination at Sarajevo; 1914. Photo: Paul Popper

14 Recruitment in Berlin; 1914. Photo: Ullstein Bilderdienst

15 Enlistment in Britain. Recruits with sergeant. Photo: Imperial War Museum

16 'Your country needs you.' Photo: Imperial War Museum

17 Painting by C.R.W. Nevinson: *The Harvest of Battle*; 1919. Photo: Imperial War Museum

18 German artillery troops on horseback passing through Brussels in 1919. Photo: Imperial War Museum

19 German troops going up to the front by light railway, Menin. Photo: Imperial War Museum

20 Allied merchant ships being attacked by a German U.35; April 1917. Photo: Imperial War Museum

21 German troops in gas masks making an assault supported by a gas cloud. Western front. Photo: Imperial War Museum

22 Lord Northcliffe on a visit to the Italian front; 1916. Photo: Associated Newspapers Limited

23 Drawing by George Grosz: *Fernsehen*. Photo: Südd. Verlag Bild-Archiv

24 Anti-German riots in the East End of London; June 1915. Photo: Radio Times Hulton Picture Library

25 General Joffre, President Poincaré, George V, General Foch, Sir Douglas Haig at Beauquesne; 12 August 1918. Photo: Imperial War Museum

26 Lord Kitchener leaving the War Office. General Sir William Robertson behind. Photo: Radio Times Hulton Picture Library

27 The Kaiser conferring with Hindenburg and Ludendorff. Photo: Imperial War Museum

28 German retreat to the Hindenburg Line. British troops crossing the Somme at Brie; 20 March 1917. Photo: Imperial War Museum

29 The Tank fortress of Vaux just before the victorious Germans attacked; June 1916 (Verdun). Photo: Ullstein Bilderdienst

30 Clemenceau. Photo: Collection Viollet

31 Lloyd George; c. 1917. Photo: Vandyk

32 Women in industry. Traying bullets at Woolwich Arsenal. Photo: Imperial War Museum

33 Unveiling of the colossal wooden statue of Hindenburg, Siegesallee, Berlin; 4 September 1915. Photo: Imperial War Museum

34 Siegfried Sassoon. Photo: Faber and Faber, London

35 Henri Barbusse. Photo: Radio Times Hulton Picture Library

36 Romain Rolland. Photo: Radio Times Hulton Picture Library

37 Pacifist meeting in London; 28 July 1917. Photo: Topix, Thomson Newspapers

38 Bolshevik poster. Photo: John Freeman

39 Bolshevik poster. Photo: John Freeman

40 Von Kuhlmann signing the Treaty of Brest-Litovsk, while Count Czernin of Austria-Hungary looks on. Photo: Imperial War Museum

41 General Foch. Photo: Collection Viollet

42 British tank of the First World War. Photo: Imperial War Museum

43 War memorial, Beaux-Arts, Paris. Photo: Collection Viollet

44 War memorial by Hugo Lederer; 1926. Humboldt University, Berlin. Photo: Ullstein Bilderdienst

45 Royal Artillery memorial, Hyde Park Corner, London. Photo: National Monuments Record

46 The Grande Place, Ypres, showing the ruins of the Cloth Hall and Cathedral; summer 1916. Photo: Imperial War Museum

47 The cortège of the unknown soldier on its way to Westminster Abbey after the unveiling of the Cenotaph; 11 November 1920. Photo: Gernsheim Collection

48–49 German currency in the inflation of 1922 and 1923. Radio Times Hulton Picture Library

50 Painting by Sir William Orpen: *The signing of the peace of Versailles*; 28 June 1919. Photo: Imperial War Museum

51 National Theatre, Prague. Photo: Czechoslovak Travel Bureau (Orbis)

52 Ernst Barlach: Beggar and peasant woman. Figures carved for St Catherine's, Lübeck. Photo: Thames and Hudson Archive

53 Leoš Janáček: Manuscript of the score of the opera *The Adventures of Fox Sharpears*. Photo: Courtesy Orbis, Prague

54 The Auditorium of the Grosses Schauspielhaus, Berlin, by Hans Poelzig; built 1919. Photo: Marburg

55 Starving people waiting for bread in the Russian famine of 1921. Photo: Radio Times Hulton Picture Library

56 Lenin in the presidium of the First Congress of Comintern in the Kremlin. Fotokhronika Tass

57 Sidney and Beatrice Webb. A contemporary portrait.

58 Still from the film *Aelita* with sets by Rabinovitch and costumes by Alexandra Exter; 1919–20. Photo: Camilla Gray

59 Still from *Battleship Potemkin* by Eisenstein. Photo: National Film Archive

60 Stage production of 1922 by Meyerhold of *The Death of Tarelkin* with sets by Vavara Stepanova. Photo: Society for Cultural Relations with the USSR

61 Nurses casting their votes; December 1918. Photo: Radio Times Hulton Picture Library

62 Stanley Baldwin at the time of the General Election; 1922. Photo: Radio Times Hulton Picture Library

63 Flower garden frocks modelled at Ascot; 1928. Photo: Radio Times Hulton Picture Library

64 Dr Stresemann in Oslo, where he received the Nobel Peace Prize in 1926. Ullstein Bilderdienst

65 Mussolini making a speech; 22 August 1928. Photo: Topical Press

66 Fascist celebrations, November 1923. Cyclists saluting Mussolini. Photo: Radio Times Hulton Picture Library

67 Franz Masreel: *Die Passion eines Mensches*. Woodcut.

68 Coal strike at Wigan; April 1921. Miners in the market-place. Photo: Radio Times Hulton Picture Library

69 Emergency transport during the general strike; 1926. Steam lorry and trailer bring City workers to the Bank of England. Photo: Radio Times Hulton Picture Library

70 The Austin Chummy Tourer; 1925. Photo: BMC, Birmingham

71 Morris Oxford two-seater; 1925. Photo: BMC, Cowley

72 Morris Cowley two-seater; 1925. Photo: Nuffield Organization, Cowley

73 Berlin tramcar of the 1920's. Photo: Südd. Verlag Bild-Archiv

74 Strand traffic scene; August 1923. Photo: Radio Times Hulton Picture Library

75 Hydro-electric station, Mühleberg, Switzerland; built 1921. Photo: Swiss National Tourist Office

76 Alcock and Brown in front of their aeroplane a few days after their Atlantic flight; 1919. Photo: Radio Times Hulton Picture Library

77 Shayle Gardener and Hubert Carter speaking into a transmitter at Marconi House; February 1923. Photo: Radio Times Hulton Picture Library

78 A typical interior of the 1920's with radio. Photo: Radio Times Hulton Picture Library

79 Rudolph Valentino. Photo: National Film Archive

80 Mary Pickford. Photo: National Film Archive

81 Still from *The Gold Rush* with Charlie Chaplin. Photo: National Film Archive

82 Interior of the Granada, Tooting; built 1931. Photo: Ian Yeomans, *Sunday Times*

83 Beaverbrook in the 1930's. Photo: *Daily Express*

84 Exhibition of paintings by D. H. Lawrence at the Warren Gallery, London, which was raided by the police. Photo lent by Philip Trotter

85 D. H. Lawrence by Jan Juta. Photo: National Portrait Gallery, London

86 Aldous Huxley. Photo: Bassano and Vandyk Studios, London

87 T. E. Lawrence. Drawing by Augustus John. Photo: National Portrait Gallery, London

88 Sylvia Beach and James Joyce in her bookshop in Paris. Photo: Gisèle Freund

89 Ernest Hemingway in Paris. Portrait Study by Man Ray. Photo: Ullstein Bilderdienst

90 Gertrude Stein. Portrait by Picasso. Metropolitan Museum of Art, New York

91 Siegmund Freud. Photo: Ullstein Bilderdienst

92 C.G. Jung. Study by Karsh of Ottawa. Photo: Camera Press, London

93 Albert Einstein. Photo: Ullstein Bilderdienst

94 Painting by Salvador Dali: *Apparition of a face and fruit dish on a beach*, Wadsworth Athenaeum, Hartford, Connecticut. Photo: Anna Wachsmann

95 Painting by Max Ernst: *Fruit of a long experience*. Collection Roland Penrose, London. Photo: John Webb, London

96 Arnold Schoenberg by Egon Schiele; 1917. Photo: Thames and Hudson Archive

97 Alban Berg by Arnold Schoenberg; 1920. Vienna, Historisches Museum der Stadt Wien

98 Anton Webern by Oskar Kokoschka. Photo: Thames and Hudson Archive

99 Bela Bartók. Photo: Courtesy Hungarian News and Information Centre, London

100 Percival Mackey's jazz band rehearsing on a roof garden in London with the dancer Monte Ryan. Photo: Radio Times Hulton Picture Library

101 Invitation to a Bauhaus costume party; 1928. Photo: Museum of Modern Art, New York

102 Painting by Paul Klee: *Architektur (Gelb-violett gestufte Kuben)*; 1923. Hermann Rupf, Berne

103 Painting by Wassily Kandinsky: *Yellow Accompaniment*; 1924. Solomon R. Guggenheim Museum, New York

104 Teapot by M. Brandt; 1924. Photo: Museum of Modern Art, New York

105 Chair with frame of nickel-plated steel tubing by M. Breuer; 1925. Photo: Thames and Hudson Archive

106 Igor Stravinsky by Picasso; 1917. Photo: Thames and Hudson Archive

107 The Bauhaus building at Dessau. Photo: Ullstein Bilderdienst

108 Luigi Pirandello. Photo: Italian Cultural Institute, London

109 André Gide by William Rothenstein. Photo: Courtesy Penguin Books, Harmondsworth

110 T.S. Eliot by Wyndham Lewis. Harvard University, Cambridge, Mass.

111 Marcel Proust. Portrait by J.E. Blanche. Photo: R.B. Fleming

112 Kurt Weill. Photo: Ullstein Bilderdienst

113 Bertolt Brecht. Photo: Ullstein Bilderdienst

114 *Man is Man*, a Berliner Ensemble production of Brecht's play. Photo: Ullstein Bilderdienst

115 Painting by Ben Shahn: *The Passion of Sacco and Vanzetti*: 1931–2. Whitney Museum of American Art

116 Sir Oswald Mosley being cheered by his constituents after his victory at Smethwick in 1929. Photo: Radio Times Hulton Picture Library

117 Hunger-marchers in London; October 1932. Photo: Keystone

118 Painting by V.M. Vladimirsky: *Denikinites fleeing from Novorossiisk*. Fotokhronika Tass

119 Children in a Nazi demonstration; Munich, 1925. Photo: Ullstein Bilderdienst

120 Hitler with Hess and other friends during his imprisonment at Landsberg, Bavaria. Photo: Imperial War Museum

121 Hitler greeting Hindenburg in front of the Berlin State Opera, 'Volkstrauertag' 25 February 1934. Photo: Ullstein Bilderdienst

122 Painting by Richard Klein: *The Third Reich*. Photo: Ullstein Bilderdienst

123 The *Reichsparteitaggelände* in Nuremberg by Speer. Photo: Ullstein Bilderdienst

124 Haile Selassie of Abyssinia addressing the League of Nations in 1935. Photo: Südd. Verlag Bild–Archiv

125 The burning of the Reichstag; February 1933. Photo: Imperial War Museum

206

126 Burning of books by Nazi students in Berlin, May 1933. Photo: Ullstein Bilderdienst

127 Pickets placed outside Jewish-owned stores in Germany; 1933. Photo: Gernsheim Collection

128 Karl-Marx-Hof (now Heiligenstädterhof), Vienna. Photo: Bildarchiv de Öst. National-bibliothek, Vienna

129 Painting by Pablo Picasso: *Guernica*. Mural; 1937. On extended loan to the Museum of Modern Art, New York. Photo: Museum

130 Greta Garbo. Photo: National Film Archive

131 Max Reinhardt and Lady Diana Manners in his house chapel at Schloss Leopoldskron; 1924. Photo: Ullstein Bilderdienst

132 Edward VIII announcing his abdication to the nation. Photo: Keystone

133 Paris Exhibition; 1937. General view with German and Russian pavilions. Photo: Collection Viollet

134 The Munich Peace Conference. Chamberlain, Daladier, Hitler, Mussolini and Ciano; October 1938. Photo: Imperial War Museum

135 Hitler declares war in the Reichstag; 1 September 1939. Photo: Ullstein Bilderdienst

136 Proclamation of war at the Royal Exchange, London; 4 September 1939. Photo: United Press International

137 Käthe Kollwitz: 'Nie Wieder Krieg!' Poster of 1924. Photo: Thames and Hudson Archive

138 German soldiers march through Warsaw; October 1939. Photo: Imperial War Museum

139 Allied soldiers being evacuated from Dunkirk. Photo: Imperial War Museum

140 Liddell Hart. Photo: Elliot and Fry Ltd, London

141 Marshal Pétain broadcasting the beginning of the winter campaign. Photo: Collection Viollet

142 The main gate of Auschwitz concentration camp. Photo: C.A.F., Warsaw

143 Belsen victims. Photo: Imperial War Museum

144 Churchill and Bevin inspecting G.H.Q. Northern Command Battle Training School; 1942. Photo: Radio Times Hulton Picture Library

145 Painting by Herbert Agricola: *Battle in the ruins of Monte Cassino*; 1944. Bavarian National Museum (Army Museum), Munich. Photo: K.N. Kempter, Munich

146 Painting by John Piper: *Somerset Place, Bath*. Courtesy the Trustees of the Tate Gallery, London

147 Sketch by Henry Moore: *Shadowy shelter*; 1940. Graves Art Gallery, Sheffield. Published by permission of the Sheffield Corporation

148 Damage to Coventry after a raid in 1940. Photo: Radio Times Hulton Picture Library

149 Hamburg after a raid; July 1943. Photo: Ullstein Bilderdienst

150 German forces on a battlefield between Tobruk and Sidi Omar. Photo: Imperial War Museum

151 Soldiers and officers help free a snowed-in train, Central Russia; 1941. Photo: Südd. Vorlag Bild-Archiv

152 Churchill with Stalin in the Kremlin. USSR newsreel photo; 1942. Photo: Imperial War Museum

153 President Roosevelt declaring war against Japan after Pearl Harbor; 7 December 1941. Photo: Imperial War Museum

154 D-Day troops assembling on the beach, 6 June 1944. Photo: Imperial War Museum

155 General de Gaulle. Photo: Collection Viollet

156 Marshal Tito with his cabinet ministers and supreme staff. Photo: Imperial War Museum

157–158 Yugoslav partisans in 1944. Photos: Imperial War Museum

159 The Soviet flag being raised on the Reichstag, Berlin, 8 May 1945. Photo: Deutsche Fotothek, Dresden

160 Hitler's bunker; Berlin, 1945. Photo: Ullstein Bilderdienst

161 The corpses of Mussolini and Clara Petacci in the Piazzale Loreto, Milan, 29 April 1945. Photo: Keystone

162 Truman, Stalin and Churchill at Potsdam for talks; 17 July 1945. Photo: Imperial War Museum

163 Dresden in ruins after the heavy air-raids of 1945. Photo: Ullstein Bilderdienst

164 Rebuilding Dresden; 1966. New buildings in the town centre. Photo: UBZ

165 Coventry rebuilt. The Precincts. Photo: Bryn George. Camera Press

166 Map: post-war Europe. Drawn by Joan Emerson

INDEX

Abyssinia, 140
Adler, F., 40
Aeroplanes, 49, 92
Alcock and Brown, 92, *76*
Alexander I, 63
Alienation, 116
All Quiet on the Western Front, 117
Alsace, 15
Anarchists, Italian, 141; Spanish, 147
Ankara, 53
Anti-Fascism, 141, 144; and Spanish civil war, 146–48; and Second World War, 157
Anti-semitism, 134, 144, 154–55
Arabs, 53
Architecture, 113
Aristocracy, eclipsed, 78–80
Armistice (Nov. 1918), 51, 58
Asquith, H. H., 34
Atlantic crossed, 92
Attila, 136
Auschwitz, monument of German civilization, 169, *142*
Austin car, 89
Australia, flight to, 92
Austria, forbidden to join Germany, 69; civil war in, 145; under Hitler, 152
Austria-Hungary, national conflicts in, 12, 14, 64; military service in, 15; in 1914, 16; parliament suspended, 17; few deserters from army of, 38; Pope and, 40; strikes in, 47; disintegrates, 52, 68; aristocracy of, 79; produces comic masterpieces, 116; and Russia, 126
Aztecs, 56

Baghdad railway, 16
Baldwin, S., 78; on radio, 94–95; *62*
Barbusse, H., 40, *35*
Barnes, G. N., 38
Bartók, B., 108, *99*
Bauhaus, 113, 141, *101–3, 107*

Bavaria, Bolshevik revolution in, 60, 70
Beaverbrook, Lord, 99, *83*
Belgium, 14, 23, 24, 26, 59, 164
Belloc, H., 134
Belsen, *143*
Benedict XV, 39
Berg, A., 17, 108, *97*
Berlin, 59, 100, 115, 141, *54, 73, 159*
Bethmann Hollweg, 20, 36, 133
Bevin, E., 170, *144*
Bismarck, O., 7
Boers, 25, 31
Bolshevik revolution, 46, 78, 125; alarm, 47–48, 59–60, 69–71
Biscay, Bay of, 167
Bottomley, H., 160
Braque, G., *10*
Brecht, B., 115, *113, 114*
Brest-Litovsk, peace of, 48, *40*
British Museum, 45
Budapest, 64, 193
Bukharin, 124
Byron, Lord, 148
Byzantium, 52

Caillaux, 40
Casals, P., 148
Chamberlain, J., 134
Chamberlain, N., *78*; at World Exhibition, 152; and Hitler, 154; bleats, 155; hopes for peace, 156–57; forced to declare war, 158; as war leader, 160; *134*
Chaplin, C., 96, 148; and Hitler, 131; *81*
Charlemagne, 52
Charles, Emperor, 42
Chesterton, G. K., 134
Chiang Kai-Shek, 117
China, 64, 117, 181
Churchill, W. S., on Bolshevism, 72; and unconditional surrender, 162; partnership with Bevin, 170; embraces Soviet Russia, 180; and Roosevelt, 182; and Stalin, 191; at Potsdam, 192; *144, 162*

Numbers in italics refer to illustrations

209

Cinema, 96, 97, *82*
Clemenceau, G., 36, 63, *30*
Colonial empires end, 140
Comintern, founded, 70, 71, 73; resigned to waiting, 86; impotence of, 126; dissolved, 126; Dimitrov, head of, 143; *56*
Communism, victory of, in Russia, 46; and Social Democrats, 74; Depression brings no benefit to, 122–23; transformed by five-year plan, 126–28; failure of, in Germany, 135; glories of, displayed at World Exhibition, 152, *133*; democracy allies with, 180; not driving force of Russian war, 184; and de Gaulle, 185; in Yugoslavia, 187; suspicions of, 191; in eastern Europe, 193; American fears of, 196
Concentration camps, 143, *142, 143*
Confessions of Zeno, 116
Constantinople, 52; greatness ends, 53
Covent Garden, 90
Coventry, *148, 165*
Cubists, 17, 107, *10*
Cyprus, 84
Czechoslovakia, 64; democratic, 86; German minorities in, 141; dismembered, 154, 157; falls apart, 155; Germans expelled from, 192
Czechs, 38
Czernin, *40*

Dada, 115
Daladier, E., at Munich, 154, 156; as war leader, 160; *134*
Dali, S., 116, *94*
Dawes plan, 86
Democracy, 76–77
Denmark, 69, 160
Depression, Great, 119–20; and socialism, 122–23; and Fascism, 129, 135; and United States, 138; prosperity despite, 148, Devonshire, Duke of, 79
Dictionary, Concise Oxford, 7
Dictionary, Shorter Oxford, 7

Disarmament Commission withdrawn from Germany, 86
Dresden, *163, 164*
Dunkirk, 165, *139*

Ebert, President, 68
Edinburgh, 7
Edward VIII, 151, *132*
Egypt, 33, 84
Einstein, A., 104, *93*
Eisenstein, 73, *59*
Elbe, 79
Electricity, effects of, 92–94
Eliot, T. S., 115, *110*
Ellerman, Sir J., 79
English Channel, 151; flown, 92; Germans reach, 165; effective barrier, 170
English law favours aristocracy, 79
Englishmen, whether European, 7; dine at midday, 9
English war books, 117
Ethiopia, Emperor of, 140
Europe, extent of, 7; Christian, 9; dominates world, 12; continues to dominate world, 84–85; returns to normal, 86; American loans to, 119; Soviet Russia's place in, 126; Hitler's plans for, 131; National Socialism a product of, 136; no Balance of Power in, 138; Hands off, 152–53; and Second World War, 159; dominated by Germany, 167–68; no British plans for uniting, 171; Roosevelt assumes, does not exist, 179; fate settled outside, 182; Resistance provides history for, 184; pride restored, 185; recovers, 192–93; partitioned, 196; continuing leadership of, 197–98
Existentialism, 106
Expressionism, 115, 141

Fascism, Italian, 80, 81, 83, 188; German, 130; British, 151; expansion of, 129–30; *66*
Feu, Le, 40
Fichte, 130

Five-year plan, 125–27
Flanders, battle of, 45
Foch, F., as Supreme Commander, 50; and armistice terms, 51–52; *25, 40*
Ford, H., 41, 88
Fourteen Points, 51
France, a republic, 9; shares domination of world, 12; universal military service in, 15; co-operates with Germany, 16; and First World War, 24; mutinies in army, 38; United States and, 42; nearly defeated, 43; and end of war, 50; war damage in, 59; and satellite states, 68; postwar troubles in, 80; retains empire, 84; frontier with Germany guaranteed, 86; motor cars in, 90; Hitler's plans against, 133; anti-semitism in, 134; weakness of, 138; contribution of, to World Exhibition, 152; tied to Poland, 155; wishes to yield, 157; war measures in, 160; waits for German collapse, 161; defeated, 164–66, 170; Allied landing in, 183; Resistance in, 184–85
Franco, General, 179
Franz Ferdinand, 20, *13*
Freeman, E. A., 134
Free Trade, 120–21; ends, 135
French revolution, 78, 119
Freud, S., 104, *91*
Friends, Society of, 40
Functionalism, 113
Futurists, 17

Gamelin, General, 164
Garbo, G., 148, *130*
Garibaldi, G., 83, 147, 188
De Gaulle, General, 184–85, *155*
Gide, A., 115, *109*
Gladstone, W. E., 33
Gloucester Terrace, 7
Geneva, 64, 117
George V, 6, *25*
George, D. Lloyd, 34, 43, 60, 63, 69, 121, *31*

Germany, shares domination of world, 12; universal military service in, 15; co-operates with Great Britain and France, 16; and outbreak of First World War, 20–22; war aims of, 29; political changes in, 32; United States at war with, 42; defeats Russia, 43; makes peace with Russia, 48; final effort by, 49; appeals for peace, 50; revolution in, 51; armistice with, 52; no Social Democratic majority in, 56; Bolshevik peril in, 59–60; potentially dominant, 68; and treaty of Versailles, 69; Junkers in, 79; republic, 80; Fascism in, 83; unemployment in, 86; motor roads in, 89–90; radio in, 94; war books, 117; Depression in, 119–20; streets riots in, 122; National Socialism in, 130–32; Hitler comes to power in, 135; France powerless against, 138; limited rearmament in, 140; grievances of, 140; anti-semitism in, 134, 144; aids Spanish rebels, 146; glories of, at World Exhibition, 152, *133*; greater Germany achieved, 154; invades Poland, 158; peacelike war economy in, 159–60; expected to fall down, 161; treatment of Poles by, 162–63; defeats France, 165–66; supreme, 167–68; exterminates Jews, 169; air force defeated, 172; negligible effects of bombing in, 174; attacks Soviet Russia, 180; Roosevelt and, 181; Russians do most of fighting against, 183; Resistance to, 184; Resistance in, 188–89; surrenders, 191; ruled by victors, 192; out of running as great power, 196
Gestapo, 155
Good Soldier Schweik, 116
Gorlice, battle of, 32
Great Britain, share of world dominion, 12; naval power, 15; co-operates with Germany, 16;

suffragettes in, 17; compulsory military service in, 28; political changes in, 34; war taxes, 38; United States and, 42; and knockout blow, 43; and German defeat, 50; general strike in, 60, 86, *69*; postwar troubles, 80; retains empire, 84; unemployment in, 86; million motor cars in, 89; decline of towns, 90; newspapers, 99; mass unemployment, 119; abandons Free Trade, 120; hunger-marchers, 122, *117*; Hitler's plans against, 133; withdrawn from Europe, 138; and German anti-semitism, 144; guarantees Poland, 155; stands by Poles, 157; war measures, 160; waits for Germany to collapse, 161; negative war aims of, 171; survives, 172; plans for defeating Hitler, 173; obsessed with indiscriminate bombing, 173–74, 177–78; becomes United States satellite, 181; only European power fighting against Germany, 182, diminished, 192

Great Exhibition of 1851, 152
Groener, General, 38
Gropius, W., 113
Grosz, G., *1, 23*
Guernika, 148, *129*
Guizot, 124

Haig, D., 31, *25*
Halifax, Lord, 117, 154, 156
Halles, Les, 90
Hamburg, *149*
Hardie, K., 7
Hašek, J., 116
Hemingway, E., 103, 148, *90*
Henderson, A., 38
Hess, R., *120*
Hindenburg, 31, 36, 38, *27, 28, 33*, 121
Hitler, A., and motorways, 89; character, 131, 133; and living space, 134; comes to power, 135; loathsome, 136–37; attitude of western statesmen to, 138–39; and rearmament, 140; griev-

ances of, 141; as dictator, 143; anti-semitism of, 144; Austria and, 145; and Rhineland, 151; and Czechs, 154; and Poland, 155–56; expects peaceful victory, 157; moves too fast, 158; overthrow of, demanded, 162; applies racial doctrines, 163; military genius of, vindicated, 164–65; French sympathies with, 166; supreme in Europe, 167; British and, 170–72; invades Soviet Russia, 179; involves United States in Europe, 181; attempts against, by Resistance, 188–90; death of, 191; all Germans somewhere else, 193; *120, 134, 160*

Holland, 59; radio in, 95; conquered, 167; resistance in, 185
Hollywood, 96, 148
Horse, decline of, 90–91
Hugenberg, 99
Hungary, Bolshevik revolution in, 60, 70; undemocratic, 77, 79
Huxley, A., *86*
Hyde Park, 152

Ibsen, H., 115
Impressionists, 107
India, 25, 52, 117
Inflation, 60, 83
Inquisition, 134
International Brigade, 147
Ireland, 12, 64
Irwin, Lord, 117
Istria, 192
Italy, and First World War, 23, 160; disorder in, 60; Fascism in, 80–81; guarantees Locarno, 86; motorways in, 89; and electricity, 93; radio in, 94; railway stations, 113; and Great Depression, 129–30; attempts to act against Germany, 138; conquers Abyssinia, 140; grievances of, 141; aids Spanish rebels, 146; enters Second World War, 160, 167; British plans against, 178; Roosevelt and, 181; falls out of war, 182; Mediterranean campaign

against, 183; Resistance in, 188; loses Istria, 192
It's True If You Think It Is, 106

Jacobins, 71
Japan, 12, 33, 85, 138; and Pearl Harbor, 160; defeated, 192
Jazz, 112, *100*
Jericho, 70
Jews, national home for, 53; persecution of, 134, 144; attempt to exterminate, 169
Joffre, General, 30, 31, 36, *25*
Joyce, J., 100, 115, *88*
Jung, 104, *92*
Junkers, 79

Kaiser, G., 115
Kautsky, K., 40
Kellogg Pact, 117
Keynes, J. M., 140
Kipling, R., 134
Kitchener, Lord, 31, *16, 26*
Kokoschka, *12*
Kollwitz, K., *137*
Kühlmann, *40*
Kursk, battle of, 183

Labour party, British, 72, 121, 135
Lansdowne, Lord, 40
Law, Bonar, 78
Lawrence, D. H., 100, *84, 85*
Lawrence, T. E., 100, *87*
League of Nations, proposed by Wilson, 44; set up, 62–63; and Germany, 69; Germany admitted to, 86; generally respected, 117; and National Socialists, 130; fails to save Abyssinia, 140; Roosevelt has little faith in, 181
Léger, *11*
Leipzig, 143
Lenin, V. I., 14; attitude of, to First World War, 44–45; and Bolshevik revolution, 46; makes peace with Germany, 47–48; effective against war, 56; and international revolution, 70, 72, 124; and New Economic Policy, 71; death, 73; *56*

Leo XIII, 39
Liberal party, British, 135
Liddell Hart, B. H., 165, *140*
Liebknecht, K., 40
Lindbergh, C., 92
Little Man, What Now?, 130
Locarno, treaty of, 86
London, 7; as banking centre, 9, 12
Lords, House of, 78
Lorraine, 15
Louisiana, 112
Low Countries, 160
Ludendorff, General, 31, 36, 50, *27*
Luther, M., 130

MacDonald, R., 40, 117
Mackinder, H., 134
Malraux, A., 148
Mann, T., 30
Marx, K., 122, 124, 126
Marxism, 40; Lenin's view of, 45; and Soviet Communism, 72, 74, 138
Matteoti, murder of, 81
Maxim gun, 33
Mazzini, 83
Mediterranean, 183
Metternich, 147
Meyerhold, 73, *60*
Michelin guide, 90
Milan, *2*
Milner, Lord, 48
Monaco, 9
Monash, Sir J., 31
Morris car, 89, *71, 72*
Moscow, 73, 193
Mosley, Sir O., 121, 151, *116*
Motor car, influence of, 88–90, 148
Munich, 134; conference at, 154–57, *134*
Mussolini, B., sets up dictatorship, 80, 83–84, 134; and Great Depression, 129–30; attacks Abyssinia, 140; ideological hostility to, 141; Austrian hopes of, 145; at Munich conference, 154; hopes for peace, 156; proposes conference, 158; Hitler's only equal, 167; overthrown,

182, 188–89; killed, 191; 65, *134*, *161*

Napoleon I, 26, 28, 32, 63, 163, 167, 179
Nash, J., 7
National Socialism, 58; origins of, 130; and Great Depression, 135; character of, 136, 137; dictatorship of, 143; glories of, at World Exhibition, 152; destruction of, demanded, 162, 171; *119*
Nazi–Soviet pact, 157, 161
Netherlands, 88
Nevinson, C. R. W., *17*
New Economic Policy, 71
New Order, 163, 167–69
New Orleans, 112
News From Nowhere, 124
Newspapers, 99, 148
Nicholas II, 44
Nivelle, General, 38
Northcliffe, Lord, 29, 99, *22*
Norway, invaded, 160; Resistance in, 185

Opera Houses, 9

Palestine, 53
Papen, 78
Paris, 7, 17, 38, 100; peace conference at, 62, 154; cultural capital, 103, 115; World Exhibition at, 152, *133*; opera house, *2*
Parliament Act, 78
Passports, not needed, 9; required, 86
Peace, Decree on, 46
Peace Ship, 41
Pearl Harbor, 160
Persian Gulf, 84
Pétain, 39, 144, 166, 185, *141*
Peter the Great, 126
Petrograd, 38, 44
Picasso, P., 100, 108, 148, *89*, *106*, *129*
Pickford, M., 97, *80*
Pirandello, 106, *108*
Planning, in First World War, 36–38; and Great Depression, 121–

22; in Soviet Russia, 124–26; in Second World War, 160
Poincaré, R., *25*
Poland, 12, 26, 32; German territory lost to, 69; and Russian war, 71; aristocracy in, 75; German minorities in, 141; German demands on, 154–55, 157; invaded, 158, 160; conquered, 161; German treatment of, 162–63; restored, 192
Poles, 38, 64
Portugal, a republic, 9; colonies of, 16; population of, increases, 88; at World Exhibition, 152
Positivism, 104
Potsdam, conference at, 192, 197, *162*
Pound, E., 81
Prague, 64, *51*
Prince Consort, 152
Proust, M., 115, *111*
Pudovkin, 73

Radio, 94–95, *77*, *78*
Railways, 9
Rearmament, 140
Red Army, 71
Red Cross, 25
Red Indians, 12, 163
Red Shirts, 147
Reichstag, and peace resolution, 43; and Great Depression, 135; fire, 145; *125*, *159*
Reinhardt, M., 141, *54*, *131*
Relativity, 104
Remembrance Day, 58
Renaissance, 104
Resistance, provides European history, 184; restores European pride, 185; in Yugoslavia, 187, *157*, *158*; in Italy, 188; in Germany, 188–90
Rhineland, 51, 69, 151
Rite of Spring, 17
Robertson, General, 32
Rolland, R., 40, *36*
Roman Catholic Church, and extermination of Jews, 176
Rome, 52, 56; march on, 80

Roosevelt, F. D., and New Deal, 144; not at Munich, 154; keeps Great Britain going, 178; intends to run world, 179, 181; accepts Soviet Russia, 180; co-operates with Stalin, 182; and unconditional surrender, 190; death of, 191; *153*

Russia, passports needed for, 9; military service in, 15; in trouble, 16, 17; and First World War, 24, 160; revolution in, 36, 38, 44–46; seeks peace, 42; defeated, 43; effects of war on, 59

Sacco, 117, *115*
Salvation Army, 135
Sarajevo, 20, 196, *13*
Sassoon, S., 40, *34*
Scale, diatonic, 7, 108
Scandinavia, 164
Scarborough, 26
Schleicher, General, 78
Schlieffen, General, 164
Schoenberg, 17, 108, *96*, *97*
Sedan, battle of, 165
Serbia, 20, 23
Sezession, 17, *12*
Shaw, G. B., 81, 115
Siam, 12
Siberia, 126
Social Democrats, Austrian, 145
Social Democrats, German, and First World War, 24, 29; no majority for, 56; support republic, 80; Hitler and, 132
Socialism, 14; and Communism, 76; and Great Depression, 122, 124; 141, 188; without compulsion, 172
Somme, battle of, 21, *28*
Soviet Russia, set up, 46; makes peace with Germany, 48–49; no war memorials in, 56; famine in, 62, 69; out of Europe, 68; New Economic Policy in, 71; isolated, 72; enlightened, 73; and democracy, 77; becomes respectable, 117; five-year plan in, 124–26; Comintern defends, 127; alleged

plans against, 138–39; terror in, 143; aids Spanish government, 146; glories of, at World Exhibition, 152, *133*; purge in, 153; alliance with, feebly sought, 156; pact of, with Nazi Germany, 157; remains neutral, 158, 162; attacked by Germany, 160; occupies Poland, 161, 163; invaded by Germany, 179; embraced by democracies, 180; Roosevelt co-operates with, 181–82; does most of fighting, 183; defied by Tito, 187; gains Polish territory, 192; defensive policy of, 196

Spain, 9, 76, 122; civil war in, 146–48, 173
Stalin, 9, 72–73; and five-year plan, 124–26; purge by, 153; not at Munich, 154; and Roosevelt, 182; defied by Tito, 187; supposed plans of, 190; Churchill alarmed by, 191; bestrides Europe, 192, *152*, *162*
State Department, 129
Stauffenberg, 189
Stein, G., 103, *89*
Stratford-on-Avon, 7
Stravinsky, I., 17, 112, *106*
Stresemann, G., 80, *64*
Stockholm, *4*
Sudan, 31
Suez Canal, 53
Supreme Commander, Foch, 50, *41*; Gamelin, 164
Supreme Council, 69, 71
Supreme Court, Leipzig, 143
Surrealists, 107, *94*, *95*
Svevo, I., 116
Sweden, 59, 167
Switzerland, 9, 40, 44, 64, 83, 167, 75

Talkies, 148
Tanks, 49, *42*
Tel el Kebir, battle of, 33
Tito, 187, *156*
Trieste, 15, 116
Trotsky, 14, 117

Truman, H., 180, 191; at Potsdam, 192, *162*
Turkey, passports required for, 9; not Christian, 12; empire of, disintegrates, 52; spoils of, go to Great Britain and France, 84

Ukraine, 133
Ulster, rebellion in, 17
Unconditional surrender, demand for, 162, 181, 190, 191
Unemployment, 85, 119
United Nations, 181
United States, European in character, 12; advocate peace, 40; enter First World War, 42; war aims of, 43–44; war debts to, 53, 59; not in League of Nations, 63; increased strength of, 85; barred to immigrants, 86; European independence of, demonstrated, 117; stock exchange crash in, 119; Soviet Russia behind, 126; Communist sympathizers in, 129; isolationism in, 138; Roosevelt in, 144; supposed special British relationship with, 148; remain neutral, 158; outstrip Europe, 159; enter Second World War, 160; expected to supply Allies, 162; British count on resources of, 173; not anxious to enter war, 178; pushed into war, 180; intend to run world, 181
Urals, 7

Valentino, R., 96, *79*
Valmy, battle of, 58
Van der Lubbe, 143
Vandervelde, 14
Vanzetti, 117, *115*
Verdun, battle of, 32, 144, *29*
Vienna, 17, 42, 52
Voltaire, 40

Warsaw, 7, 64, 71, 193, *138*
Waste Land, 113
Waterloo, battle of, 58
Waugh, E., 116
Webb, Sidney and Beatrice, 72, 76, *57*

Webern, A., 17, 108, *98*
Weill, K., 115, *112*
Wells, H. G., 30
West Hartlepool, 26
Wigan, *68*
William II, 20, 25, 68, *8*
Williams, V., 108, 148
Wilson, W., wants peace without victory, 41; declares war, 42; war aims of, 43–44, 55; and end of war, 51–52; at peace conference, 62–63; more Utopian than Roosevelt, 181
Wodehouse, P. G., 116
Wolseley, General, 33
Women, emancipation of, 87
World Disarmament conference, 139–40
World Exhibition, 152
World War, First, outbreak of, 20–22; conduct of, 24–27; strategy of, 28–32; increased intensity of, 33–38; transformed by entry of United States, 42–44; final phase of, 49; deaths in, 53; memorials to, 58, *43, 44, 45, 47*; effects of, 59; no balance of power after, 68; and decline of aristocracy, 78; discredits Europe, 84; and emancipation of women, 87; wireless telegraphy in, 94; newspapers during, 99; reversed, 165; 76, 112, 119, 123, 126, 129, 130, 134, 138, 141, 170, 181
World War, Second, 58, 76, 117, 126; generals in, 91; five-year plan more terrible than, 126; Abyssinia liberated during, 140; outbreak of, 158, devastating effects of, 159; spreads, 160–61; character of, determined by British policy, 173; German invasion of Soviet Russia central event in, 179; United States pushed into, 180; Great Patriotic War, 184; tames Communists, 193

Ypres, *46*
Yugoslavia, King of, 77; Resistance in, 184–85, 187; gains Istria, 192